COLD CASE

CASE

VANCOUVER

COLD CASE

VANCOUVER

The City's Most Baffling
Unsolved Murders

EVE LAZARUS

ARSENAL
PULP PRESS

COLD CASE VANCOUVER
Copyright © 2015 by Eve Lazarus

ARSENAL PULP PRESS
Suite 202 – 211 East Georgia St.
Vancouver, BC V6A 1Z6
Canada
arsenalpulp.com

The publisher gratefully acknowledges the support of the Canada Council for the Arts and the British Columbia Arts Council for its publishing program, and the Government of Canada (through the Canada Book Fund) and the Government of British Columbia (through the Book Publishing Tax Credit Program) for its publishing activities.

 Canada Council Conseil des arts   Canadä
for the Arts   du Canada

An earlier version of the material in "Vancouver's First Triple Murder" appeared in *Sensational Vancouver* (Anvil Press, 2014).

Cover photograph: Scene of Evelyn Roche murder from *Vancouver Sun*, April 5, 1958
Interior design by Lisa Eng-Lodge, Electra Design Group
Cover design by Gerilee McBride and Oliver McPartlin
Edited by Susan Safyan

Printed and bound in Canada

Library and Archives Canada Cataloguing in Publication:
Lazarus, Eve, author
    Cold case Vancouver : the city's most baffling unsolved murders / Eve Lazarus.

Includes bibliographical references.
Issued in print and electronic formats.
ISBN 978-1-55152-629-4 (paperback). –ISBN 978-1-55152-630-0 (epub)

    1. Murder–British Columbia–Vancouver. 2. Cold cases (Criminal investigation)–British Columbia–Vancouver. I. Title.

HV6535.C33V35 2015   364.1'5230971133   C2015-903475-2

CONTENTS

Acknowledgments

Writing may be a solitary endeavour, but I am extremely fortunate to have the talents of a wide range of creative and knowledgeable people to draw upon.

I owe a depth of gratitude to Dave Obee, Editor-in-Chief at the *Times Colonist* in Victoria, who braved the first read of my unedited work and generously gave me his time and guidance in shaping and making this into a much better book.

I would also like to thank the "Belshaw Gang" who were always there to help with encouragement, leads, and information—in particular John Belshaw, Tom Carter, Diane Purvey, Cat Rose, Jason Vanderhill, Stevie Wilson, and Will Woods. Thanks also to Mark, Megan, and Matthew Dunn, Arleene Ewing, Rob Howatson, Tom Hawthorn, Pamela Post, Nikki Strong-Boag, Kat Thorsen, and Steve Webb whose insights and insider information helped with different parts of the book; as well as Dr Nicole Aube, Dr Neil Boyd, Dr Robert Gordon, Corporal Gord Reid, Constable Brian Montague, and retired major crime detectives Fred Bodnaruk, Brian Honeybourn, and Steve McCartney for their expert assistance.

It would be impossible to write a historical crime story of this kind without the resources of the archives, museums, and public library. Special thanks to Kristin Hardie at the Vancouver Police Museum, to Vancouver Archives, the Vancouver Public Library, Daien Ide at the North Vancouver Museum and Archives, Carolyn Soltau at the *Sun/Province* library, and Ron Dutton, archivist at the BC Gay and Lesbian Archives.

Most of all, I'm grateful to Susan Safyan, my editor at Arsenal Pulp Press, publisher Brian Lam, Robert Ballantyne, Cynara Geissler, and book designer Lisa Eng-Lodge.

Preface

Sometimes "unsolved" murder cases are actually resolved, in that police know who did it, but they just can't close the case. There are a few reasons for this. Sometimes the suspect dies before the trial; sometimes there isn't enough evidence to bring the suspect to trial. In most provinces, police have the power to lay charges on reasonable grounds, but in British Columbia it's up to the Crown. Prosecutors will only go ahead with charges if they are convinced that there is a substantial likelihood of conviction and that it's in the public interest to pursue a charge. If, for example, the suspect is already in jail serving a life sentence for another murder, the Crown may decide that public interest would not be served by holding another trial. The problem with this is that life sentences are rarely served for life, and criminals can reoffend. The end result is that the families of the victims are not given closure. At the time of writing, the Vancouver Police Department had 337 unsolved murders on its books dating back to 1970.

Since the introduction of ViCLAS (Violent Crime Linkage Analysis System) in 1991, Canadian police are getting better at linking cases in different jurisdictions and catching serial offenders. Cases entered into ViCLAS include all solved and unsolved murders and attempted murders, sexual assaults (often a precursor to murder), missing persons where foul play is suspected, and child abductions by strangers.

Scientific improvements, especially in DNA analysis, are helping to solve murders, but it's not a panacea. DNA found at a crime scene is only useful to investigators if the suspect's DNA is already in the system. For very old cases, and before investigators understood the value of blood and secretions, much of the evidence was contaminated, lost, or even thrown out.

In the process of writing this book, a lot of people told me how much safer Vancouver was in the good old days. It's not true. Vancouver had a violent streak and a string of sexual predators. The city could be a particularly dangerous place for women, children, immigrants, and gay men.

Today, murder is relatively rare in Canada, accounting for 0.1 percent of all police-reported violent crime. And the homicide rate is falling. In 2013 it was at its lowest point since 1966. According to the Vancouver Police Department's Annual Report for 2013, the city's murder rate is among the lowest in North America and dropping. Out of 5,713 violent crimes reported in 2013, only six were murders—a drop from eight in 2012. To throw out another comparison, in 1962 the City of Vancouver had a population of less than 400,000 and notched up eighteen murders. In 2013 our population reached just over 600,000—more than a fifty-percent increase—yet the number of murders dropped to six. Nine out of ten murder victims are killed by someone they know, and the group most likely to be murdered are eighteen-to twenty-four-year-olds.

One last point. Police officers won't talk to media about unsolved cases, even really old ones. I've relied heavily on contemporary newspaper accounts, vital statistics, autopsy reports, obituaries, official police department reports, and interviews with retired major crime detectives, and family and friends of the victims. Some of these memories are seventy years old.

Introduction

A few days after *Cold Case Vancouver* was finished and sent off for editing, I received an email from Daien Ide, reference historian at the North Vancouver Museum and Archives. Daien had come into the possession of a family album with the owner's name, Miss J. Conroy, inscribed in the inside front cover. Daien was intrigued and found out that twenty-four-year-old Jennie Conroy was murdered in 1944, and her murderer never brought to trial.

Jennie is now part of my book and one of the hundreds of murders that remain unsolved in Metro Vancouver. Even when you take out high-risk lifestyles such as gangs, drugs, and prostitution, there are still dozens of random murders that are now cold, some dating back several decades. The victims are essentially invisible, forgotten by everyone except their family and friends. I wanted to write a book that would help to change that, to tell the stories of their lives, not just of their murders, and I wanted to look at their murders through a historical filter.

Some of the cases will be familiar. The story of the Babes in the Woods, two small skeletons discovered in Stanley Park in 1953, has taken on almost mythological proportions. The case offers a fascinating insight into how investigative techniques have evolved and how the development of DNA analysis changed the face of the investigation in the 1990s.

In 1947, around the estimated date when the two children were killed in Stanley Park, seven-year-old Roddy Moore was beaten to death on the way to his east side school. His family still searches for answers.

I've included the story of Danny Brent because he was the first gang murder victim in Vancouver—shot in the head by hired killers from Montreal in 1954 and left on the tenth hole of the University of British Columbia golf course. Brent's unsolved murder also brought attention to the Vancouver Police Department, to Vancouver as the drug capital of Canada, and it precipitated the Tupper Commission into police corruption and the fall of Chief Constable Walter Mulligan.

The brutal murder of Robert Hopkins, a printer living in Vancouver's large gay closet, gave me a reason to delve into what it was like to be a gay man in the 1950s.

There were the vicious murders of Evelyn Roche, David, Helen, and Dorothy Pauls, and Lila Anderson a few years later, and then the tragic abduction and murder of three seven-year-old girls killed in 1967, 1969, and 1972.

The 1970s were a particularly brutal time for young women. Louise Wise had just celebrated her seventeenth birthday when she was stabbed to death in her East Vancouver home. Debbie Roe was a twenty-two-year-old country-and-western singer from Langley, BC, recently back from cutting a record in Nashville with her sister. She was murdered coming home from work one night.

Two cases touched me personally because the victims were people whom my friends and neighbours had known. One, Brenda Young, a thirty-eight-year-old mother of four, was killed in her retail store at the bottom of North Vancouver's Lonsdale Avenue in 1976. Six months later, Rhona Duncan, a sixteen-year-old girl, was walking home from a party in North Vancouver when she was raped and murdered just a block from her home.

In 1985 Jimmy and Lily Ming were kidnapped from their Strathcona home. The killers demanded $700,000 in ransom long after they were strangled, dismembered, and left in garbage bags along the Squamish Highway. Nine years later, Nick Masee, a retired banker, and his wife Lisa went missing from North Vancouver. Nick had connections to the Vancouver Stock Exchange, which *Forbes Magazine* called the "Scam Capital of the World," and where I worked in the late 1980s.

Then in 1996, Muriel Lindsay, a forty-year-old postal worker who had recently survived cancer, was about to move into a new apartment when she was beaten to death in her West End boarding house room.

Because unsolved murders, by their nature, don't have an ending, I wanted to finish the book with a cold case that was solved. Vivien Morzuch was a fifteen-year-old French Canadian boy killed near Kamloops. The story tells the lengths that police went to in solving this case and some of the legal obstacles they faced in bringing his Vancouver-based killer to justice.

Every officer I spoke with told me of at least one unsolved murder that they worked on in which they were sure they knew who the killer was, but lacked the evidence to prove it. The truly frightening thing is that these killers might still walk around among us. As a forensic expert for the Vancouver Police Department said, even with DNA and all the scientific improvements, "we don't catch the smart ones."

In July 2015, Daien Ide, reference historian at the North Vancouver Museum and Archives, came into the possession of a photo album with the name Miss J. Conroy inscribed inside the front cover. The photos, which were dated up to 1942, were carefully placed in the album and the people in them identified by their first names. Daien discovered that the owner of the album— twenty-four-year-old Jennie Eldon Conroy—was murdered in 1944. Digging a little deeper, she discovered that Jennie's murder was never solved. The album began to take on a life of its own.

CHAPTER 1

War Worker Murdered near West Vancouver Cemetery

Jennie Conroy finished her shift as a grain loader at Midland and Pacific Elevator in North Vancouver at 5:00 p.m. on December 27, 1944. She hurried back to the little house where she lived with Winnifred Richards on East Eighth Street. She was meeting her father John Conroy and her sister Eva at her brother's West Vancouver house for Christmas dinner, and she didn't want to be late. Jennie put on a mauve and grey dress, her tan coat, black shoes, and gloves. She decided not to wear a hat and left her long brown hair loose. She dashed out of the house and reached the North Vancouver Ferry ticket office at 6:10 p.m., where she discovered that she had missed the bus to West Vancouver by less than a minute.

Jennie Conroy, North Vancouver, 1941.

George Malloch, the ticket seller, recognized Jennie and sent her to check the schedule for the next bus. "She was alone when she came to my wicket and seemed quite happy," Malloch told a reporter. "I told her to ask Albert Webber at the turnstile." Webber did not know Jennie, but later told reporters that he had given a West Vancouver timetable to a "tall, good-looking girl."

Jennie discovered she had a forty-five minute wait for the next bus.

The Conroys waited for Jennie until 8:00 p.m. When she still hadn't arrived, they ate their Christmas dinner. John and Eva left for their North Vancouver home around 10:00 p.m.

At 2:00 a.m. a worried Winnifred Richards phoned to tell them that Jennie had not come home.

Photo: Eve Lazarus, 2015

Winnifred Richards' house on East 8th Street in North Vancouver, where Jennie Conroy lived at the time of her murder in December 1944.

Slain Girl Battled Attacker, Say Police

Shortly after 10:00 a.m. on Thursday, December 28, Dave Chapman, a foreman for the West Vancouver Board of Works, and James Elliott, a municipal truck driver, were returning from the city dump. They discovered Jennie's body on a gravel road off Third Street, in an uninhabited area near the Capilano View Cemetery in West Vancouver.

She had been badly beaten, and the back of her head was smashed in by a claw hammer. Her jaw and nose were broken. There was a cut on her left hand. A spot of blood found on Third Street and gouge marks on the road indicated that she had been dragged roughly forty-seven feet (14.3 m) along the dead-end street. Vancouver police inspector John F.C.B. Vance found gravel in the ball of one of her feet and noted that the soles of her stockings were wet. He thought that this indicated that she had tried to run from her attacker, likely by jumping out of his vehicle. Coroner Dr Harold Dyer put her time of death at around 4:00 a.m. on December 27. He was unable to determine where the actual crime took place.

Police found only one of her shoes, lying near Third Street. They also found an empty whiskey bottle nearby that was soaked with Jennie's blood, her identification papers, and a West Vancouver bus time table.

The Capilano View Cemetery, near where Jennie was murdered in December 1944.

Rendezvous with Death Suspected in North Vancouver Slaying

Early in the investigation, police learned that Jennie had given birth to an illegitimate child less than three months before. The police leaked this information to the press, and the day after Jennie's body was found the newspapers reported that Jennie was an unmarried mother who had turned her baby over to the welfare authorities. One newspaper added that "a former sweetheart" was questioned by police and released when he proved he had no connection to Jennie's murder.

The news further traumatized her family, who were unaware of her pregnancy, and by portraying Jennie as an unwed mother, the investigation misled both police and the public with statements such as this one reported in the *Vancouver Sun* that: "Police have learned that the girl's activities have become 'obscure' during the past year, and believe she may have met questionable companions although her father said he did not know of any."

Police told reporters that they felt Jennie must have "met her assailant by a prearranged plan" and went with him in a car. They theorized that she had spent the night with him, and that an empty bottle of whiskey by the road indicated that they were drinking before her murder. The sub-text was that somehow Jennie deserved this.

When the truth came out, there was no apology or retraction. But her former landlady Winnifred Richards was quoted as saying: "She was a wonderful person. Everybody loved her." She told the reporter that Jennie had left the house that day in a happy mood.

When evidence emerged to prove that Jennie was not the architect of her own murder, police started to look at other theories. They found that she had bought a bus ticket to West Vancouver, had missed the bus, and was seen walking away from the terminal. They believe that she might have starting walking to the next stop, but accepted a lift along the way.

"Revenge, jealousy, anger, or some such emotion may have prompted the unknown killer to beat Jennie to death," police told the media.

Police Conduct Exhaustive Search for Slayer of Miss Conroy

This was the first murder in West Vancouver since it had been incorporated as a municipality in 1912. Working on the case was West Vancouver Police Chief Charles Hailstone, assisted by Vancouver City Police Superintendent of the Criminal Bureau of Investigation, Walter Mulligan. The newspapers called it "the most intensive man-hunt in the municipality's history."

RCMP loaned their tracker dog Cliff to scour the bush around the crime scene. The dog found a clot of blood-stained excelsior (a material used for packing) two blocks from where the body was found. The also found bits of excelsior stuck to Jennie's coat.

On the day after Jennie's murder, police found her missing left shoe, an open-toed black pump, lying on the lawn at the corner of Pender and Beatty Streets in downtown Vancouver. It suggested that the killer could have come across the inlet after dumping Jennie's body in West Vancouver, then discovered the shoe in his car and tossed it out onto the street.

Police searched for a green Chevrolet coupe that a bus driver had seen in the vicinity near the time of the murder. They appealed to laundries all over Metro Vancouver to report any blood-stained clothing brought in for cleaning, and garages were asked to be on the lookout for cars or trucks seen with traces of blood on their exterior or upholstery.

The Conroy family ca. 1925, 475 Crescent Street, North Vancouver. Jennie is second from right, front row.

Jennie Eldon Conroy

Jennie was born in North Vancouver on July 9, 1920 to Minnie and John Cecil Conroy. That year the family lived in a house on Crescent Street, a North Vancouver street that no longer exists, and they stayed there until Minnie's death from cancer six years later. John, a deckhand with North Vancouver Ferry, moved his family—Mabel, fifteen, Sid, twelve, Jennie, six, and Eva, four, to a house on East 17th Street.

By 1934, Jennie was five-foot-eight and slim, with brown curly hair and blue eyes. She attended Ridgeway Elementary but left school after grade seven to take care of the house and of her younger sister Eva. Her father was now a night watchman for North Vancouver Ferries. Sid had already left home, and Mabel had recently married and moved to Victoria.

During the war, Jennie worked as a pipefitter's helper at North Vancouver Ship Repairs, earning $100 a month. She moved out of her father's house and boarded with Winnifred Richards on East Eight Street. Winnifred's older sister Josephine worked with Jennie at the shipyards, and Winnifred's husband was away fighting in the war. Jennie's co-workers described her as a "cheery, popular girl" who was "always smiling and joking." She loved music, and she played the Hawaiian guitar. They all said that, to their knowledge, Jennie had only ever had one boyfriend. She worked at the shipyards until April 30, 1944, about the same time that her pregnancy would have started to show.

Jennie met Graham Wainright (name changed) through her job at the shipyards. The handsome twenty-three-year-old was over six feet tall, with dark hair and dark brown eyes. He was Jennie's first boyfriend. They started going out to dance or see a show once a week. When Jennie told him she was pregnant in February 1944, Wainright told her that the baby wasn't his and that she must have been "running around" with someone else. Wainright moved to Victoria, and they didn't see each other again.

In some respects North Vancouver is still very much a small town. In 1944 it was tiny. Everyone knew each other, and even though Victorian sensibilities may have softened during the war years, being an unmarried mother was still considered scandalous. Jennie had managed to save up enough money from her job at the shipyards to support herself during the pregnancy, hide her condition, protect her family from scandal, and arrange for the adoption of her baby.

Courtesy North Vancouver Museum and Archives

Jennie and Eva Conroy, early 1940s.

Jennie's baby was born on October 10, 1944. She registered her baby's birth on November 23, placed her in foster care, and shortly after went to work as a grain loader.

There is a note on the adoption file dated November 13, 1944 from a child-welfare worker stating that Jennie was determined that her baby be adopted. Wainright still denied paternity, which initially held up the adoption process. He eventually signed a paternity admission to enable the adoption, but later said that he had only done so under duress.

The child welfare worker's impressions of Jennie were included in the adoption file: "She has blue eyes, and

is neatly dressed. She appears to have a pleasant personality, and has a particularly attractive smile. Worker feels that the mother is within the normal group
of general intelligence. She was quite embarrassed throughout the interview,
and has a rather appealing shyness about her. She seems truthful and is most
sincere in her desire that the baby should be adopted so that she would have 'a
regular home with a father and mother.' She does not feel that she has enough
to offer the baby, and is particularly afraid that when Cherry reaches school
age she might be teased unmercifully by her school mates if she remained with
the unmarried mother."

Jennie would have been well aware that unmarried mothers were not
accepted in polite society. In the early 1940s, unmarried mothers were
viewed as "fallen women" and their children identified as illegitimate. "It was
considered very shameful, and certainly for middle-class and working-class
women, it would have been seen as a tremendous threat to the respectabilities
of their families," says feminist historian Dr Veronica Strong-Boag.

A doctor who attended the birth noted that Jennie was of "average
intelligence," and that the baby also seemed "normally intelligent." As Stong-
Boag explains, an unmarried mother was seen as socially contaminated or
questionable. "The assumption was that only morally promiscuous women
would become pregnant, and certainly the psychologists of the day would
suggest that this was commonly a product of low intelligence," she says. In
other words, adoption was not considered safe because it was thought that the
mother's probable low IQ and loose morals could be passed along to her baby.

Cherry Lynn Conroy

When Cherry was nine months old she was adopted by the Ward family in
Chilliwack and her name was changed to Mary Elizabeth Catherine.

"I always knew I was adopted, and I knew the name of my mother because
my adopted mother had saved the newspaper article with a picture of her in it,"
says Mary. "When I was eighteen, I went to the University of Victoria and while
I was there, I went to the BC Archives and got a copy of my birth certificate."

Mary finished university, married Brian Monckton, and the couple moved
to New Zealand where they raised five sons.

In the late 1990s, following the death of her adoptive mother, Mary decided
to find her biological family. The Ministry of Children and Family Development
provided Mary with a thick file of notes pertaining to her adoption, but they
blacked out the name of her father. In 1944 the practice was to leave the
father's name off the birth certificate if the parents weren't married. But with

help from Joan Vanstone, the founder of a search organization called Parent Finders, Mary managed to track him down to an address in North Vancouver. He admitted to knowing Jennie, but denied that he was the father of her baby, refused to take a DNA test, and asked her to never contact him again. She learned that he had married but never had children.

In 2004 Mary travelled to Canada to meet her mother's family. Sid's wife Lorraine told Mary how much she had liked her mother. "Lorraine was fond of Jennie. She told me that she was quiet like Sid, not one to be outgoing but friendly and warm," says Mary. Lorraine told Mary that Jennie had had no training and had kept the house for her father for some years. "The children brought themselves up," Lorraine told her.

Sid and Lorraine's daughter Debbie says Mary's visit was good for her father, who died in 2012. "When my family met Mary, it was quite healing in a way," says Debbie. "She's a lovely person and she was quite open about all of this."

Courtesy North Vancouver Museum and Archives

Jennie Conroy, seated second from end above "Extra trip 7:00 p.m." sign, 1942.

The Conroys

Debbie Conroy was born in 1957, thirteen years after her aunt's murder. She was the youngest of Sid and Lorraine's three daughters. Debbie found out about her aunt when she was going through the family's photo album as a child. "I asked my dad who it was and he told me her name and my mum filled me in on the rest of the story," says Debbie. "It came up again when I was in my late teens when the newspaper published something about unsolved murder mysteries and I saw the name Conroy in the paper. My dad and I talked about it again, but he was not forthcoming with details."

It wasn't until 2004, when Mary came to Canada to meet her family, that Debbie discovered that she had a cousin. "When I found out about Mary, I was a little bit surprised. I thought, Dad, couldn't you have said something about that? It was almost like he'd closed that off."

Shortly after his sister's murder, Sid sold the house he'd built on Inglewood Avenue in West Vancouver and moved his family to BC's Interior. Partly it was to try his hand at ranching, partly it was to get away from the media attacks on his sister and her horrific death. "I don't know why my dad kept so quiet, whether he felt shame," says Debbie. "I thought, How dare the press imply that it was her fault? Women were blamed for so many things."

Police Rapped in Conroy Case

A small consolation for the family came in March 10, 1945 when the *Vancouver Sun* reported that police were given a good verbal spanking by the legislature thanks to women's groups who were outraged that police would provide private details of Jennie's life as grist for the media. "Tendency on the Part of Police Departments to Compete with Each Other for Glory in Solving Crime," read the headline. The Attorney General was urged to set policy for police to stop them from giving out details that were "sordid" and "unnecessary" in the investigation of a crime.

After making headlines for a week, Jennie's murder disappeared from the papers. Then on February 2, 1945 Attorney General Maitland announced that the provincial government was offering a $1,000 reward for information that would help arrest Jennie's murderer. And while much had been made of the blood-soaked pad of excelsior found near the crime scene, nothing more was said about it until January 1952 when the *Province* ran an interview with Sergeant Don Matheson.

He Would Stake Life on Case

Matheson said he had first heard of Jennie's murder when he was overseas with the Royal Canadian Air Force. When he returned from the war, he joined the West Vancouver police and was put to work on the investigation. He told the *Province* reporter that he had continued to be obsessed with the case even after he had left the police force.

Matheson decided to take a closer look at the excelsior. He discovered that it was a type of padding that was made partly from newspapers and was manufactured in San Francisco. There were only a handful of importers of the product in Canada. His investigation honed in on a North Vancouver grocer who sold fruit and vegetables door-to-door. Although the man's name never appeared in a police report, Matheson said he had actually asked about the progress of the murder investigation during the course of two visits to the police station in the weeks that followed the murder.

Matheson followed the green grocer as he went out on deliveries in his truck and found that he made frequent crossings across the Lions Gate Bridge down Pender Street past Beatty, and could have easily tossed the shoe from his truck window.

It's possible that Jennie could have known the grocer, at least by sight. He lived in the area, visited dozens of houses through his work, and may have been someone that she wasn't threatened by, making it possible that she would have accepted a ride with him after missing her bus. Matheson speculated that the grocer, who was thirty-three and married when Jennie was killed, made a pass at her once he had her in the truck and became angry when she started to struggle with him.

"I believe he hit her on the face and ... her head hit hard against something that inflicted the injury on the back of her head and knocked her out—maybe a large bolt head on a partition behind the truck seat," Matheson told the reporter, adding that he believed that the grocer then stretched her out in the back of the truck, putting her head on the excelsior padding.

In a follow-up story a few days later, the reporter interviewed West Vancouver Police Chief Charles Hailstone and Vancouver's Chief Constable Walter Mulligan—both of whom had worked on the case in 1944. Both denied seeing Matheson's evidence.

"There were many many leads, but it was by far the most baffling case of my experience," said Chief Mulligan, who three years later would flee to California in the middle of a Royal Commission into bribery and corruption charges at the Vancouver Police Department.

When Mary contacted the West Vancouver police in 2004 for an update on her mother's murder file, she was told that the department had lost the file in 1980. Debbie says that in the more than seventy years that have gone by since her aunt's murder, police have never once contacted the family. "I believe that the police brushed it under the carpet because it was a woman who was murdered. They were a family without much means, and there was shame and blame," says Debbie. "I think her investigation was probably bungled and dropped, and I feel she is owed some justice for that."

Sources:
North Shore Press: December 29, 1944; February 2, 1945
Vancouver Sun: December 29, 30, 1944; March 10, 1945
Vancouver News-Herald: December 29, 1944; January 2, 3, 4, 1945
Vancouver Daily Province: December 28, 29, 30, 1944; January 4, 1945; January 7, 1952

The years after World War II were tough on women in Vancouver; they lost decent-paying jobs to returning veterans as more than 20,000 people flooded into the city from all over Canada in search of work. In 1946, 600 homeless and unemployed war vets occupied the second Hotel Vancouver, and newspapers reported on their "shameful conditions." Given the housing shortage, lack of a social safety net, and the choice between badly paid retail and domestic jobs, the future for women, particularly single mothers, looked bleak.

CHAPTER 2

Babes in the Woods Case Still Haunts City

In 1953, Albert Amos Tong was working with a Vancouver Parks Board crew clearing dense bush in a remote part of Stanley Park. He had been in the area now for several weeks as part of a fire hazard reduction program. As Tong was going about his work, he stepped on a lump buried under a bundle of leaves and heard a loud crack. As he raked away the leaves, he found that the cracking sound had come from a skull. And as he carefully lifted away an old coat, he saw what would later be revealed as two human skeletons.

Tong had worked for the City of Vancouver for eleven years. On the day that he found the skull and bones, he finished his shift and went home to his Eton Street house. He was busy, he said later, and he wanted to think about his discovery. The next morning he called police.

Eve Lazarus photo, 2015

On the day in January 1953 that Albert Tong found human bones in Stanley Park, he went home to his house at 2510 Eton Street to think about his grisly discovery before reporting it to police the next day.

Tong's delay in reporting his grisly find to police—whether he thought that he might have been implicated in some way or for some entirely different reason—is unknown, but it was just one of the many baffling and often bizarre details that emerged over this decades old, and apparently unsolvable, murder case.

Mystery Skeletons Found under Logs in Stanley Park

Tong's discovery in the woods that winter morning set off a chain of events that would confound the city for the next six decades.

Vancouver police sergeant Bud Errington and police constable Bill Lindsay were first on the scene. They used their hands to scrape off rotting leaves, mold, hemlock needles, and a couple of years' worth of deciduous leaf layers to unearth what was left of two children, one slightly smaller than the other. While roots from the trees had grown around and through the bones, they could see that the smaller skeleton lay face down beside a decayed log, a leather air-force style flying helmet still attached to the tiny skull. Both skeletons had black leather belts encircling what were once their waists, and identical brown, rubber-soled oxford shoes were attached to their feet.

The larger skeleton was lying across the feet of the other, and the remains were covered by a woman's coat. There was another flying cap near the right of the body, and what remained of a pair of goggles. An adult woman's brown penny loafer lay between the larger skeleton and a rotted log. A child's blue metal lunch box with a white bottom and two handles lay between the bodies. The remnants of that last lunch had degenerated to wet, fibrous tissue. Found close by—and soon to take on a prominent role in the case—was a small hatchet with a broken handle of the type commonly used by campers and roofers.

Almost immediately, the media dubbed the victims the Babes in Woods, and the case quickly took on mythical proportions—Vancouver's own Hansel and Gretel fairytale, a dark edge to the city's beloved Stanley Park, but with an unsatisfying, inconclusive ending.

Were the children unwanted and dumped and then murdered by a stranger? Or—the theory favoured by investigators—were they unwanted encumbrances lured to the park by their mother and then beaten to death with her hatchet?

After the skeletons were discovered, police boxed up the bones, gathered up the clothing and other items found at the scene, and took them to the city morgue where they were examined and reassembled by Dr T.R. Harmon, a pathologist, and the coroner, Dr John Whitbread. Harmon determined that the children were aged between seven and twelve. After a further examination of the holes in the skulls—one in the larger and two in the smaller—he determined that

Adapted from the Province, March 20, 1998

Lions Gate
Bridge

Bodies
Found ✖

Beaver
Lake

Stanley
Park

The X on the map shows
where the skeletons
were found just north
of Beaver Lake.

Courtesy Vancouver Police Museum

Where the bodies were found. Crime scene photo of Stanley Park, January 1953.

they were not made by rodents or other wild animals but by the hatchet found at the scene. The blade of the hatchet was about four inches (eleven cm) across and fitted neatly into the fractures. One child had a chop wound that matched the sharp edge of the hatchet, while the other had fracture wounds that might have been caused by the hammer end.

And even though the skeletons were wearing boy's outfits, and it was already difficult to determine sex from skeletal remains, the original case file said that one was "probably a girl." Somewhere along the way, the "probably" was dropped, and this mistake sent detectives off on the wrong track for the next forty-five years as police searched for a missing brother and sister.

Murder Reconstruction to Take Many Months

With no missing person's reports to help with identification of the bodies, police contracted Erna Engel-Baiersdorf, a renowned forensic anthropologist. Baiersdorf was also a painter and a sculptor and a prestigious anthropological reconstructionist. Before she was dispatched to Auschwitz in 1944, and later Buchenwald concentration camp, she had worked on the staff of the natural history museums in both Budapest and Vienna and was, at one time, the curator of the natural history museum in Pécs, Hungary. Baiersdorf survived the atrocities of the camps, and shortly after her release moved to Vancouver and began work at the Museum of Vancouver.

Baiersdorf, who was one of the few scientists living in Vancouver trained in forensic anthropology, was given the broken and decomposed skulls as well as the information from the medical examiner so that she could cast likenesses of the children's faces. While an exact reconstruction was impossible, Baiersdorf

Courtesy Vancouver Police Museum, Province photo March 20, 1998

Forensic anthropologist Erna Engel-Baiersdorf, shown with likenesses of the two children in 1953.

believed that the children were of a Nordic race, maybe Swedish or Norwegian. From the physical and medical evidence she was given, she concluded that the "girl" had brown hair, a prominent lower jaw, a slender build, and cavities in her teeth. The "boy," she thought, was sturdy and had dark brown hair. "The skull will show a definite facial outline—chin, jaw, bridge of nose, forehead, cheekbones," she told reporters. "The soft parts of the face can vary. Things like lips, tips of noses, and ears."

While the plaster casts were being made, police tried to recreate the clothing worn by the children. The 1953 annual report from the Vancouver Police Department described the process: "The bones were carefully gathered as were the roots, leaves, soil, and evidence in the immediate area. In the laboratory the roots were carefully separated and numerous small pieces of clothing recovered. After repeated cleaning it was possible to state with confidence the clothing worn by the children at time of death."

Police borrowed an outfit from a department store similar to the ones they believed the children to have worn, based on the scraps of clothing found on the skeletons. A photo in the annual report shows a store mannequin the size of a small child wearing a Canadian-manufactured, red Fraser tartan jacket, beige corduroy pants, brown shoes, and the aviator helmet. The leather aviators' caps, worn by boys pretending to be World War II pilots, were commonplace at the time and sold in stores for $1.59. The boys' shoes sold at Woodward's Department Store.

The woman's coat was a size sixteen and had what was called "leg of mutton sleeves." It was a cheap style of coat with a dyed muskrat fur collar, made in 1943. From the size of the coat and the woman's shoe that police found near the shoulder of one of the skeletons, investigators determined that the woman was a short and stocky five-foot-three, weighing between 125 and 135 pounds (56.7 and 61.2 kg).

Courtesy Vancouver Police Museum

Reproduction of clothing thought to be worn by one of the children. Vancouver Police Department annual report 1953.

Pinpointing Time of Death

Detective Clarendon (Don) MacKay was appointed to head the investigation team. Now that he had determined the cause of death, MacKay needed to establish an approximate time of death, which he believed would help him find the identities of the two missing children.

Detectives looked at the layers of leaves and pine needles that covered the skeletons and determined that death had taken place six years earlier. Discovering that the rubber-soled shoes that the boys wore were available only after the war years helped to fix the year of death at 1947.

After the plaster casts were complete, police circulated photos of the likenesses and the mannequin dressed in reproductions of the clothing the children were thought to have worn to newspapers across the country and asked anyone who had seen a woman with a young boy and girl in Stanley Park in 1947 to come forward. National media coverage of the crime was extensive, and tips poured in from all over North America.

While more than 100 people said they remembered seeing a boy and a girl in the park in 1947, MacKay found one report particularly convincing. A West Vancouver woman told him that she and her fiancé, an air force pilot, visited Stanley Park in October of that year. She remembered the day clearly because they fought, she told MacKay, and she broke off their engagement. She had kept a detailed diary of that time period, and her entry on that day included a story about a woman who was walking in the park with two small children, wearing a fur coat, and carrying a small hatchet. She described what the kids were wearing, and she said she remembered the two children with "remarkable clarity."

The witness, who asked that her identity remain secret, said the woman she saw in the park had dark hair, a fair complexion, and spoke to the children in a soft, low voice, calling the boy either Ronnie or Rodney. The witness and her then-fiancé had continued to walk toward Prospect Point, and on their walk back later that afternoon, she said that she saw the woman running from the old zoo cages. This time, the woman had no coat and was wearing only one shoe. She was also alone.

Because of the clothing, which she described down to the aviator-style leather caps, the estimation of the date of death, the ages of the children, and what MacKay thought was a credible eyewitness account, police focussed their murder investigation on October 5, 1947.

Babes in the Woods Slain by Mother?

MacKay thought the murderer was a woman because of the strength of the blows. "They were light blows that barely made a depression in the skull," MacKay told a reporter in 1953. "I believe a man would have struck harder."

From the evidence and the eyewitness testimony, MacKay believed that either the children's mother or a guardian had struck the children down from behind, rolled the younger child between the log and a vine maple, and dragged the elder child's body across his legs. She then covered their bloodstained bodies with her coat, either through remorse or because it was too difficult to bury them in the ground. In his scenario, the woman found her shoe trapped between the older child and a log, and when she jerked her foot free, the shoe stayed behind as she fled from the bloody murder scene.

MacKay suspected that the mother had killed her children and then committed suicide. Murder-suicide was certainly a plausible theory. The years after the war were rough on women, particularly single mothers who lost decent-paying jobs when veterans returned and men flooded in from Eastern Canada and the Prairies in search of work. Vancouver was in the throes of a housing shortage, and judging by the headlines of the day, crime was escalating. Often, women's only option was working in badly paid retail or domestic jobs, and the long hours and low wages left few options for child care.

The 1948 annual report for the Vancouver Police Department mentioned a population increase of 22,000 and seven murders in which three involved

Vancouver Police Detective Don MacKay, outside his home at 29th and Main Street in 1929.

Photo courtesy Rob Zylstra

mothers and children. "In two of which, a mother shut herself in a room with a child and committed suicide by gas, the other being where a mother threw her two children off a bridge."

Who Were the Babes in the Woods?

Tips flooded in from members of the public who remembered someone with children of those ages in 1947 and whose present whereabouts were unknown. MacKay checked every one. He traced seventy-six pairs of children who were unaccounted for in Western Canada, finding some as far away as Scotland and Australia.

MacKay worked almost exclusively on the Babes in the Woods case for the next three years. He needed to know why someone would use an axe to murder two children, dump their bodies in Stanley Park, and cover them with a woman's coat. "Well, I suppose you could pretty well say I was obsessed by it for about three years," MacKay told a reporter in 1986. "I had two children about those ages at the same time, so I guess it kind of got to me."

While MacKay searched through missing persons' records, police contacted local school boards to find out if a boy and a girl, probably brother and sister, had failed to return to school around 1947. Social agencies were also asked to check their records for any children of similar ages who may have been on their caseloads at that time. Police checked out each lead, personally setting eyes on each child and ensuring their safety. MacKay devoted himself to the case; he compiled birth records, talked with school boards, and consulted other police departments.

One tip led to a girl and boy who couldn't be found. MacKay zeroed in on Madeline Fortier, a French Canadian from Lévis, a small town in Quebec. Fortier was, at one time, the mother of a boy and a girl who matched the estimated ages of the Babes in the Woods. She had been in Vancouver in the fall of 1947 and told authorities that she had her children adopted out. MacKay desperately wanted to check on this lead, but his superiors wouldn't give him permission to travel to Quebec. MacKay died thinking that he had solved the case.

By 1960, police still had no clue as to the identity of the two children or their murderer.

Coroner Glen McDonald told reporters that no plans had been made to bury the two children, because burial would destroy the physical evidence and any hope of ever identifying the children through their medical histories and records. The bones of the children and the artifacts recovered at the scene were stored in three file boxes and left in the basement of Vancouver's Coroner's Court on

East Cordova Street with other unsolved case files. And there they remained for the next two-and-a-half decades.

Interest was revived in 1984 when anthropologist Mark Skinner decided to work on the case with his forensic anthropology class at Simon Fraser University. Skinner and his students determined that the children were actually fraternal twins, and their different sizes were accounted for by different biological growth rates, not their ages. Using X-rays of the children's jawbones, classified in the lab as 9101 (the male) and 9102 (the female), the class worked on the assumption that they were the same age—six or seven—because both children were at exactly the same stage of tooth development. While it was an interesting theory, it proved to be another red herring in the ongoing murder mystery.

Over the life of the investigation, police had filed away boxes of tips about a missing girl and boy, and twelve psychics had also offered assistance, including a Buddhist monk who told police that the boy and girl were originally buried in the walls of his house.

One of the strangest details to emerge over the years is the connection with serial child killer Clifford Olson. As Kerry Gold, a *Vancouver Sun* reporter, wrote in 2003: "Olson was seven at the time of the murders and living on Lulu Island in New Westminster. His mother was one of the tipsters who'd come forward after the bodies had been discovered. She told police that her neighbour's children had gone missing."

Tenacious Investigator May Crack Vancouver's Ultimate Cold Case

The case stayed dormant until 1996 when the RCMP joined with various municipal police forces to form the Provincial Unsolved Homicide Unit. Detective Sergeant Brian Honeybourn, a veteran cop with twenty-eight years on the force, was put in charge of five detectives and given the freedom to choose which cases he would reinvestigate.

Honeybourn was born in New Westminster in 1947. He had been raised on stories about the Babes in the Woods case by his parents, and he was fascinated by the fifty-year-old murder. He decided to order up the case from the archives, blow the dust off the files, and take another look. The report from the initial investigation was just two pages long.

"You could tell these were the days before acid-free boxes," he said. "The old file was made up of onion skin paper and carbon paper, and a lot of the pages looked like they'd been attacked by mice. To this day I can't tell you if that file was complete or not. There are a lot of things I don't know."

In 1998, Honeybourn went to the Vancouver Police Museum and packed up all the bones and exhibits that were on display. He discovered that the rest of the children's bones had been placed in a cardboard box in a police warehouse. Honeybourn, who had a budget that his predecessors could only have dreamed about, took the remains to Dr David Sweet at the University of BC. Dr Sweet, an internationally renowned expert in forensic dentistry, had developed a process of extracting DNA from teeth—the last parts of the human body to decompose. At a cost of $10,000, Sweet extracted two teeth from the skulls, decontaminated them to remove the DNA of anyone else who might have handled the remains, froze them, and then pulverized the teeth to create a talcum-like powder, used chemicals to expose the cells, and sliced the membrane to release DNA into a solution where it could be analyzed.

DNA Tests Destroy Theory in Long-Ago Child Killings

"David [Sweet] phoned me about three weeks later while I was up in Kelowna working on another case," Honeybourn recalls. "He says, 'Brian are you sitting down?' and I asked why. And he says, 'Because the bones are of two little boys, not a boy and a girl.'"

The results revealed the presence of X and Y chromosomes, proving the children were both male. DNA also revealed that not only were the boys not twins, they had two different fathers. Sweet's findings immediately lifted the suspicion from Quebec's Madeline Fortier, who had a boy and a girl, and effectively tossed out nearly a half-century of police work. Honeybourn believes that MacKay would have cracked the case decades ago if he'd had the information that the skeletons belonged to two little boys.

"Had we known at the time they were both boys, it might have made a world of difference," he said. "I wonder how many people called up the Vancouver Police Department in those days and said, 'We know where there are two boys that are missing,' and some policeman on the other end of the line said, 'Well, we're looking for a boy and girl, thank you very much.' I can guarantee this went on."

Investigators Shift Gears

Like Don MacKay before him, Honeybourn believed that the boys were killed by their mother in a planned yet frenzied killing. There was nothing on the hands of the boys to indicate defensive wounds, which was not surprising, says Honeybourn, given their young ages and the speed with which the bludgeoning would have taken place. "When you get a skull injury like that you get a terrific loss of blood immediately," he says. "It was very quick, and death would have been pretty instantaneous."

Honeybourn and Sweet were able to confirm that the hatchet, which had taken on such an ominous role in the media, was indeed the murder weapon. But while many pointed to its presence as evidence of premeditated murder, as Honeybourn points out, back in those days, it wasn't unusual for people to carry hatchets in Stanley Park to cut up kindling for their wood stoves. A shingler's hatchet or leather axe was typically used when installing cedar shake roofs, and the buildings around Stanley Park were primarily cedar shingle and shake construction.

Honeybourn also wasn't convinced about the date of the murders. When he reinvestigated the story of the West Vancouver woman who kept a diary and broke up with her fiancé in the park, he found out that she had lied. Honeybourn says he doesn't know why she lied—perhaps it was a way of injecting herself into a story that was getting so much attention—but all the information needed to make her story credible was found in the newspapers of the day, and her lie threw off the year of death. The original investigators had fixed on 1947 as the most likely year of death largely because of the woman's report—and a completely haphazard and unqualified examination of the crime scene. Today police would lock down a crime scene for days, trying to find and preserve every piece of evidence, take site surveys, and photograph every inch of the scene, but back then the forensic examination would have been a few black-and-white photos and a couple of cardboard boxes to hold the evidence.

"Everything was wrapped up on the scene in one day," says Honeybourn. "They counted leaves and deciduous matter that had fallen on the ground—you can't really go by that. There was no botanist called in. That was just the best guess." There was also no easy way to tell how badly the scene had been disturbed by the Parks Board staff in the area, or even how much damage Tong had done when he stepped on and ultimately discovered one of the skulls.

Another theory that had helped pinpoint the date was the boys' shoes. Police had originally thought that the shoes were imported from Asia only after World War II. Honeybourn discovered that the shoes were available in Vancouver prior to the war.

It meant that the actual murders could have occurred years earlier.

New Theories

Armed with the new information, Honeybourn's team went back through the case files looking for tips referring to a missing set of boys. What looked like a promising lead concerned a woman who lived at the New Foundation Hotel on Cordova Street with her two boys in the 1940s. "One day, the boys disappeared.

We looked ... and found out through social services that, in fact, those boys were still alive in 1961."

Searching back through the original case file, Honeybourn found a solid lead from a logger who said that he and a friend had picked up a red-haired woman hitchhiking with two small boys who were wearing flying helmets near Mission in 1947. He'd driven them through Stanley Park, he said, and eventually dropped them off there. Because he had reported a set of boys, his evidence wasn't investigated.

Honeybourn tracked down the logger. The man, by this time aged seventy-five, told him that the woman had a record for prostitution. She was concerned that social services was going to take away her children. Honeybourn found a local who remembered a woman who fit the description, and said she lived on Cherry Street in Mission, BC. With the help of former CKNW radio reporter George Garrett, he eventually tracked her down only to find that while she had died in Abbotsford, her boys had grown up and were very much alive.

Another theory that looked promising, says Honeybourn, involved a teacher named Lawrence Samuel Smith who wrote to police in 1953 about something odd he saw in Stanley Park in 1947. Smith, a biology teacher at a secondary school in Revelstoke, BC, wrote that he was collecting ocean specimens for his class. He told police that he remembered seeing a woman walking with two small children along the seawall toward Brockton Point in early January of 1947. He says he noticed them because one of the children was banging on the pipe rail along the edge of the path with a hatchet.

Later, Smith said, he walked around the park to some benches overlooking Beaver Lake where he found a "hysterical woman" sitting on a bench while a man "paced back and forth." He said the woman had blood on her leg, was wearing only one shoe, and wasn't wearing a coat, even though it was quite cold. He says she told him that she had fallen into a ditch, scraped her leg, and lost her shoe. After investigating the lead, Honeybourn found that Smith was in Stanley Park in 1951, not 1947, and the bones had been there years longer.

At the time of writing, Honeybourn was interested in two other leads. In the first, a report in the police file told how a young sailor visiting from Esquimalt on Vancouver Island was on the seawall with his fiancée in May 1944. He saw a woman jump out of the woods in front of him wearing only one shoe and no coat. The woman, he said, made a guttural sound and ran off.

Stanley Park

In 2014, TripAdvisor named Stanley Park the "top park in the world," and it's not hard to see why. It's a 1,000-acre urban park almost entirely surrounded by water. While 8 million people visit Stanley Park every year, most of them stay along the seawall, the beaches, and the children's play areas; few venture into its dense forest, parts of it untouched for centuries.

There's always been a dark side to Stanley Park—it's just kept hidden by the majestic trees and primitive forest. It's the part of the park where the squatters, homeless, and mentally ill live, where criminal transactions take place, and probably where bodies stay buried.

Back in the 1940s, when the Babes were murdered, Vancouver could be a violent place. Daily newspaper reports told of armed robberies, sexual assaults, suicides, and murder. In May 1945, Olga Hawryluk, a twenty-three-year-old waitress, was found beaten to death in English Bay. She'd been killed by a soldier. In July 1946, Garry Billings, eleven, was murdered by a soldier and dumped off the Bridle Path from Second Beach. And in June 1947—the same year the Children's miniature railway that runs through the park was completed—South Vancouver resident Hilda Norma Burton, twenty-seven, was found raped and strangled near Lost Lagoon. Two years later, the park witnessed "the Lovers' Lane marauders," a series of brutal beatings and violent rapes by a group of men posing as police officers from the morality squad.

The two little boys known as the Babes in the Woods were found by the entrance to the old Orville Fish Hatchery near Beaver Lake. In the nearby West End and Coal Harbour neighbourhoods, the population has burgeoned, and huge skyscrapers dot the landscape. But the trail where the boys were found—less than 164 yards (150 metres) from the main park drive where it hairpins up from the waterfront toward the Lions Gate Bridge, and where thousands of cars commute across the bridge every day—still feels remote.

Another lead comes from a retired Vancouver policeman named Ron Amiel. Amiel, who was born in 1930, grew up in Vancouver and knew the family of the signalman at Prospect Point in Stanley Park. The family left the lighthouse in 1935, but the woman, who lived for a time with Amiel's grandmother in the West End, was allegedly a prostitute and had two young sons whom Amiel was told had gone missing.

Honeybourn's hope is that the two little boys found in Stanley Park will be identified as DNA analysis becomes more sophisticated. "I don't care if the janitor solves it," says Honeybourn. "I'd just like closure for these little boys."

Kids' Skulls Displayed for Years at Police Museum

Once Sweet had extracted the DNA, Honeybourn decided he didn't want the children's skulls to remain on display at the Vancouver Police Museum; he felt it was disrespectful. At one point, Honeybourn said, the exhibit with the children's bones even went on display at Vancouver's annual Pacific National Exhibition.

Honeybourn saved some of the remains for future scientific analysis and had the rest of the bones cremated. Without the knowledge of his superiors, he arranged a simple service for the children in May 1997. He and a police chaplain took the police boat from Vancouver's Granville Island out to Kitsilano Point, and he tipped the ashes into English Bay at the entrance to False Creek. The annual Vancouver Children's Festival was taking place in the same area at that time, and Honeybourn said that this added a nice touch to the ceremony.

Honeybourn left the police force in 2001. And just like Don MacKay before him, Honeybourn has taken the Babes in the Wood with him into retirement. He is under no illusion that the killer will ever be found and brought to justice—he believes that it was the mother, and that she is long dead. But he keeps several binders of material at his home to occasionally leaf through and look for new ideas. The Babes still live on at the Vancouver Police Museum. And although the skulls are now just replicas, the display, which includes the hatchet, the helmet, the shoes, and black and white crime scene photos, is a chilling reminder of this unsolved case.

Sources:
Georgia Straight: September 18, 1997
Globe and Mail: January 16, 1953; April 2, 1960; April 27, 2004
Ottawa Citizen: March 22, 1998
Province: January 15, April 15, July 17, 1953; March 20, 1998; October 10, 2014
Vancouver Sun: May 6, 1998; August 11, 2003
West Ender: October 20, 1983

In 1947, Vancouver was still in flux after the war. There were a lot of transients as young men poured in from all over Canada in search of work. The city experienced a housing shortage, boarding houses sprang up, and people lived in squatting communities around the city. Roddy Moore was one of six people murdered in Vancouver that year.

CHAPTER 3

Who Killed Roddy Moore?

Seven-year-old Roddy Moore had moved to Vancouver with his mother Nettie just three months before he was murdered. He was settling into grade one at Begbie Annex School in Vancouver's Renfrew area, and seemed happy to walk the few blocks to his school alone, especially now that Nettie was eight months pregnant. It usually took the little boy about ten minutes each way, and he came home for lunch every day.

On the morning of Friday, October 17, 1947, Roddy waved goodbye to his mother and left by the front gate. It was pouring rain. Roddy walked down East Eighth Avenue until the road dipped and then up again to Rupert Street. In the 1940s, there were only four houses on the west side of Rupert, while across the road the land was still undeveloped; mostly bush skirted what is now Thunderbird Elementary. In 1947, nine houses lined East Seventh Avenue between Rupert Street and the school, where the school's soccer field sits today.

Normally, Roddy would cross Rupert Street and then continue along East Eighth to the school. But on this particular day he met up with a young friend, and they decided to race each other the rest of the way to school. His friend took the regular way to school while Roddy took the trail through the bush that the kids often used as a shortcut.

When Roddy didn't come home for lunch, his worried mother phoned the school. They told her that he hadn't arrived, but was probably just playing hooky and would turn up later that day. When he failed to come home, a panicked Nettie phoned police.

Albert Lockwood was one of the first people to join the search for Roddy on the day that he went missing. The Lockwoods lived less than a block from Roddy's home, and Albert's young son Tommy and Roddy were friends. The search for Roddy continued all weekend, and by Sunday morning, Albert was joined by dozens of volunteers searching through the scrub and looking for any trace of the little boy.

DISCOVERERS of the body of Roddy Moore in East End bush at 12:35 p.m. Sunday were Albert H. Lockwood, 3277 East Eighth, and Billy Young, 15, of 6319 Commercial Drive, a John Oliver student. Lockwood thought at first he had found a dog buried under dried bracken; he looked again, it was the murdered lad, missing from his home since Friday morning.

Hunt Called Off

Hope Dims For Mother In North Van

By Sun Staff Reporter

NORTH VANCOUVER, Oc 20. — Organized search wa called off today after a three day hunt for Mrs. Janet Linnel 34, mother of five-month-ol twins, missing from her hom in Garden Avenue since Thur day.

Chances of Mrs. Linnell sti being alive in the Capilano Can yon area are considered ver slim.

The Vancouver Sun covered Roddy's murder in detail in 1947. Above: Roddy's grave is marked with a stake by Det.-Sgt. F.O. Fish. Top right: Albert H. Lockwood and Billy Young discovered Roddy's body. Bottom right: Joyce Jensen was the last person to see Roddy alive.

Day of death started descent to self-made hell

From A4

the Moores forbidden subjects.

That persisted for years until, inevitably, the family ghosts reappeared. But by then John Turner's descent into a self-made hell

Turner eventually returned to Nettie but within a year he would sell his interest in the mill and move to Nelson where he found a job in a mine. Nettie joined him in January, 1950, with two children and pregnant with a third, Patricia, who was born

Top left: Roddy's grave is marked with a stake by Detective-Sergeant F.O. Fish.
Top right: Albert Lockwood and Billy Young discovered Roddy's body.
Bottom right: Joyce Jensen, 12, told police that she saw Roddy enter the bush where his body was later found.

Albert and his friend Billy Young, a fifteen-year-old John Oliver Secondary School student from the area, were poking through the bottom of a deep trench near the search headquarters at Roddy's school. The area had been combed through three times already, and Albert didn't expect to find anything. But something caught his eye as he stepped over the hollow, and he pushed back the bush with his foot. At first Albert thought he had found a dead dog buried under dried bracken. He looked again and saw that it was a boy wearing a brown wool jacket.

Roddy had lain in that shallow grave, just three blocks from his house, for more than two days. One side of his head bore the imprint of a steel heel plate, his skull was smashed, and one of his ears severed. It was found under his body when police lifted him up.

As police interviewed family and other witnesses, they were able to piece together his movements on the morning he went missing.

Except for his murderer, twelve-year-old Joyce Jensen may have been the last person to see Roddy alive. Her little brother was in the same grade as Roddy, and she recognized him talking to two younger boys. Then she saw Roddy run into the bush by himself.

Police thought they had caught a break when Gertrude Braden, who lived nearby on Rupert Street, told them that she'd heard someone scream, "Don't, oh please, don't" just after 9:00 a.m. on Friday. "I heard children's voices outside. Then a shout—sort of long and drawn-out," she told a reporter. "It sounded terrified and stopped immediately. It sounded like someone trying to stop something." It frightened her, she said, and she went to the basement to check on her grandson Billy, but he was playing, and she didn't think to call police.

About an hour later, Gertrude saw a man aged between twenty-five and thirty, dressed in work clothes, walking south on Rupert. "It was a dull and very depressing morning," she told the reporter. "The man was wearing a short tan raincoat and trousers of somewhat the same colour. He looked at me very nervously and glanced about in a furtive manner."

Police Seek Pervert or Sadist
While Roddy had not been sexually assaulted, police believed he was grabbed by a pedophile soon after entering the trail. The actual murder occurred about ten minutes after Roddy had been stopped, and police believe that this was the time used to seduce him before attempting a sexual assault. The theory went that when Roddy screamed it panicked his attacker, and the killer flew into a rage, smashing in the little boy's head with a shingler's axe.

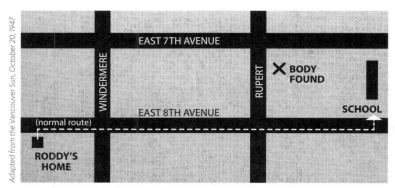

Adapted from the Vancouver Sun, October 20, 1947

Map showing where Roddy's body was found in relation to his house and school, 1947.

Roddy's twisted body lay on his right side. His school books lay by his outstretched right hand next to an envelope with "Roddy" printed in blue crayon. His shirt front was torn open, his left hand was clenched, and his knees bent as if in a sitting position. His head was shoved into the ground.

The official cause of death on Roddy's death certificate was "compression of brain with hemorrhage due to fractures of skull—lacerations and contusions of skin, face and scalp." Dr S.A. Creighton, the pathologist, believed that one severe blow knocked Roddy to the ground, cutting the left side of his face. He was then beaten on both sides of the head. At the autopsy, the pathologist found at least ten different wounds on various parts of his head. Dr Creighton determined that the multiple blows to the head could have been caused by the same instrument—either the blunt, rectangular end of a hatchet or a rock.

Police organized a thorough search of the area, looking for a murder weapon or any clue to the killer's identity. Volunteers included eighty high school students who were told that they were looking for a "blunt triangular hatchet."

Police scientist Inspector John F.C.B. Vance scoured the crime scene, taking blood and earth samples, but dozens of searchers, reporters, and photographers had already trampled all over the area, destroying any forensic evidence that the rain had failed to wash away.

A photo on the front page of the *Vancouver Sun* shows Detective Sergeant Fred Fish pounding a stake into the ground with a hatchet to mark the spot where Roddy's head had been on the ground. Another detective looks on, hand on his thigh and hat pushed back on his head.

Roddy's Family
John Roderick Moore (Roddy) (1939–1947)
Mother: Natalie Melissa Moore/Turner (Nettie) (1914–1973)
Stepfather (1): Lemuel Edward Moore (Len) (1890–1978)
Stepfather (2): John Harvie Turner (1912–1980)
Mother of John Turner: Alice Williams Hooper (1887–1961)
Sister and oldest of Nettie's thirteen children: Leona Moore (1932–)
Stepsister: Patricia (Patty) Turner (1950–)

Family Secrets
Born on November 23, 1939, Roddy was a slight, dark-haired, friendly little boy. He had blue-grey eyes and long lashes and a small but prominent scar over his right eye.

His mother said he was scared of the dark and wary of strangers. His classmates described him as a shy, quiet little boy, and they would have been surprised to learn that he had seven siblings back in Saskatchewan.

Roddy's mother, Nettie Moore (née Nickerson) was born in Ship Harbour, Nova Scotia, in 1914. She moved west at age eleven, when her widowed mother took a job as a housekeeper for Lemuel (Len) Moore, a farmer and road grader who lived in a small settlement in northern Saskatchewan. At eighteen, Nettie was carrying the forty-three-year-old Moore's baby, and they married soon after. Leona was born in 1932. By the time Nettie turned thirty-one, she had eight children. "I don't think it was a love match," says Leona. "My grandmother made him marry her and that was that."

Len worked with the highways department in North Battleford, a town more than 125 miles (200 km) away, and would be gone from home from May until October. Nettie was left to raise the children in a two-bedroom log cabin with no electricity, telephone, running water, indoor toilet, or money. "We always had lots to eat, we didn't starve," says Leona. "We always planted a huge garden and Dad would kill a cow or a pig and we had turkeys and chickens. We just didn't have money. Everybody around us was in the same predicament, it was no big deal."

One morning in June 1945, Nettie got up, packed her bags, took Roddy, and left. She moved in with her friend Jessie Hall, who lived in Meadow Lake, Saskatchewan, about fifteen miles (twenty-five km) away. Nettie's seven other children went to live with their grandmother and were eventually parcelled out to different relatives.

Leona, who now lives in Maple Ridge, BC, was thirteen the last time she saw Roddy and fifteen when he died. She believes that her mother took Roddy with her because, while Len was the father on his birth certificate, his actual father was a Métis man who would subsequently be referred to—in police reports and by Len Moore—as the "half-breed." "From the very beginning, Dad said Roddy wasn't his," says Leona.

When her friend Jessie's husband landed a job in a sawmill in Westbridge, BC, the following year, Nettie and Roddy went with them. Nettie got employment as a cook for forty dollars a month, and she and Roddy moved into a shack. She met and quickly hooked up with John Turner, an Englishman from Sheffield who worked at a logging camp. Nettie became pregnant, and when she was closer to term, Turner wanted her to be near a hospital. He sent Nettie and Roddy to live with his mother Alice Williams Hooper, who ran a boarding house in East Vancouver. Roddy and Alice quickly bonded. The little boy thought of her as his grandmother, and she was devastated by his death.

Probably because Nettie was eight months pregnant and deeply distressed, it was Turner who talked to the press and signed Roddy's death certificate. "Back home in Westbridge, the little fellow's greatest enjoyment came from fishing in the Kettle Valley River," Turner told a reporter. "He only caught one about as long as your finger, but he was really proud of it."

Turner, who told reporters that he was a partner in the Zamora Sawmill at Westbridge, said Roddy had asked to go back to Westbridge with him two weeks before. "But there would have been no one to look after him while I was working."

Turner was hardly the benevolent stepfather he claimed to be. It was soon revealed that he had beaten Roddy and often forced him to sleep on the floor of the bunkhouse when they lived in Westbridge.

Stepfathers under Suspicion

As police started to investigate Roddy's murder and his background, suspicion fell on his two stepfathers: Len Moore and John Turner. Moore was in hospital in North Battleford at the time and was eliminated from the investigation. Turner had been working in Westbridge, almost 285 miles (460 km) away, and only heard that Roddy had disappeared the day after he went missing. He took the train to Vancouver and arrived a few hours after Roddy's body was discovered. Witnesses collaborated Turner's movements on the day of and the day after Roddy's murder.

While both Moore and Turner had a motive for killing Roddy, the murder did not appear premeditated. Roddy's movements that morning were random,

Vancouver Sun, September 30, 2006

Patricia (Turner) and Leona (Moore) hold a photo of their half-brother Roddy Moore, murdered in 1947.

and police believe that he met his killer not far from the entrance to the trail. Police continued their investigation going door-to-door and interviewing dozens of neighbours, family, known sex offenders, and older school students who were missing from class on the Friday of the murder.

After just a couple of days of being front-page news, Roddy's murder quickly disappeared from the newspapers. Possibly this was because of the lack of leads, but more likely because even though the murder of a small child shocked the city, it was just one more act of violence at a particularly violent time. Earlier in the year, Vancouver police officers George Oliver Ledingham, aged thirty-nine, and Charles Boyes, thirty-eight, were gunned down and killed while trying to stop a bank robbery. The *Vancouver Sun* reported that it was just the "latest development in the all-out war between members of an apparently well-organized underworld and fighting-mad city police." According to the newspaper: "In less than two days after Chief Constable Walter Mulligan's warning that the 'gloves are off' in a war against city crime, Vancouver has had seven burglaries, two holdups, one of them armed, two attempted robberies, and nineteen thefts."

It was Mulligan's first year as police chief, and his concern was mostly centred around the transportation strike, which started on October 20, 1947—the day after Roddy's body was discovered—and lasted until November 18. "The resources of the department were taxed to the utmost handling the tremendous volume of automobile traffic on city streets during that period," Mulligan wrote in the police department's 1947 annual report.

Vancouver was still in flux after the war; there were a lot of transients in the city, young men who poured in from all over Canada in search of work. The city was experiencing a housing shortage; 2,635 boarding houses such as Alice Hooper's had sprung up, and people lived in squatting communities in areas all over the city.

Murder-alarmed Parents Fear Slayer Lurks in Bushes

In 1947 Vancouver's Renfrew area was still a long way out of the city and surrounded by bush. The patch of undeveloped land where Roddy's body was discovered had seen problems in the past. The year before Roddy died, police had warned children not to walk through the bushes near the school after reports of child molestations increased. Parents told reporters about attempted abductions, and it seemed as if nearly every family in the area had a story about a close call with a molester and one of their children.

One man told reporters that his seven-year-old son Leonard was offered a dime to go into the bush with a man just a few months before the murder. Another resident told reporters that his small daughter Ruth Marie had been chased on several occasions by a man dressed in dark clothes, wearing a hat, and carrying a cane. The mother of nine-year-old Donald, also a student at Begbie Annex School, said her son had told her a man was hanging about the school trying to coax children into the bush about a week before Roddy's murder. "Parents in the district were so worried last year that they reported the matter to police and an officer did come out, but he didn't get anyone," the woman told a reporter.

Others talked about a hobo jungle less than half a mile (one km) from where Roddy was killed, and this seemed to be confirmed when a searcher found two comforters and a blanket in bush not far from where Roddy was found. They had been stolen from the clothesline behind Agnes McKay's cabin nearby at the Hollywood Auto Court two weeks before.

Yet even with all these reports of attempted molestations, it took the murder to galvanize the neighbourhood into action. Parents organized a convoy system to see their children safely to school and back. They took out their fear on the undeveloped land and petitioned Mayor Charles Jones to clear the bush, threatening to take to it with flame-throwers if he did not. It was enough to motivate the city, and crews quickly stripped everything back to ground level.

Life after Roddy

Roddy didn't just disappear from the media; all traces of the little boy were obliterated from the Turner household. It was as if he had never existed. Three weeks after Roddy died, Nettie gave birth to Alice. The little girl was named after John's mother, and she was the first of what would eventually be five Turner children. Patty Turner was born in 1950, three years after Roddy died. Like her other brothers and sisters, she grew up not knowing either that she'd lost a half-brother or that she had seven half-sisters and brothers still in Saskatchewan.

By 1960, Alice Hooper had sold her boarding house and was living with the Moore family in a house on East Pender Street. One day, ten-year-old Patty was looking through some boxes in the basement when she came across one marked "Roddy." The box contained some sympathy cards and photos of a young boy. One of the photos showed the boy with Patty's grandmother on a streetcar, and the other showed the little boy holding a cat. When she asked her parents about him, she was told that it was none of her business. "Roddy was never spoken about in our house," says Patty.

Patty says that shortly after that, her father and grandmother got into a fight. "I can't remember what the fight was about," she says. "My grandmother lived in the front bedroom of the house. She went into the bedroom and all of a sudden she came out and she said, 'I hope you rot in hell, John, for what you did to Roddy.'" After the fight, Patty says her father threw his mother out of the house. Alice moved into a rooming house and died the following year, aged seventy-four, and things deteriorated even further in the Turner family.

Nettie got a job as a cook on the *Northland Prince*, a passenger boat that went to Alaska, and she was now gone for much of the time. Patty and her father fought constantly, and when she was twelve, she was put into foster care. She never lived at home again.

Later, when Patty asked her mother once again to tell her who Roddy was, Nettie told her he was her older brother who had died in an accident. She never talked about Roddy's death again.

When Leona Moore, the eldest of Nettie's thirteen children, moved to Vancouver, reconnected with her mother, and met the Turner clan, Nettie's second family finally learned about all of their half-brothers and sisters in Saskatchewan. But it wasn't until after Nettie died from cancer in 1973 that Patty finally discovered the truth about Roddy from Leona.

Patty immediately suspected that her father, John Turner, a gambler and an abusive alcoholic, had either murdered her half-brother or hired someone else to do it. But if John Turner knew more about Roddy's death, he never spoke about it to his family.

In 2006 Patty contacted *Vancouver Sun* reporter Gerry Bellett and told him her story. Bellett facilitated a meeting with Sergeant Chris Fielding, head of homicide for the Vancouver Police Department. Because the case was unsolved, Fielding wouldn't let them see inside the file—"dog-eared and yellow with age and barely five cm [two inches] thick," wrote Bellett, but the officer did answer some of their questions. "This is the kind of case that gives us nightmares," Fielding told them. "Even with all the advances, they may not have a better result at solving the murder today. These are the hardest cases to solve."

Over the last six decades, the area around Rupert Street has undergone a huge transformation. Houses now line both sides of the street, Alice's boarding house has been replaced by a new house, and a house sits on the spot where Roddy's body was found all those years ago.

While more than sixty years have passed without resolution for the family, and against all evidence to the contrary, Patty Turner believes she knows the name of Roddy's killer.

"Deep in my heart, I still believe my father had something to do with it," she says.

Sources:
Globe and Mail: October 20, 21, 22, November 4, 1947; August 24, 1953
Province: October 20, 21, 22, 1947
Vancouver News-Herald: October 20, 1947
Vancouver Sun: October 18, 20, 21, 22, 1947; September 29, 30, October 2, 28, November 23, 2006

"The murder of Daniel Brent on September 15," wrote Chief Constable Walter Mulligan in the Vancouver Police Department's annual report for 1954, "revolves around a narcotic ring and was part of a plot to obtain control of the narcotic distribution in this city."

CHAPTER 4

Vancouver's Drug Wars

Sam Bale, the twenty-year-old greenskeeper at the University of British Columbia golf course, was horrified when he came to work on the morning of September 15, 1954 and discovered that a car had been driven across the west edge of the green and left deep furrows in his carefully manicured grass. Sam followed the tire marks and found Danny Brent's bullet-ridden body dumped near a clump of bushes, just west of the tenth green.

He called the police.

Danny was lying on his right side, his forearms and hands folded under his chest. He was wearing a red plaid shirt, grey trousers, argyle socks, and brown shoes. Stuffed inside his shirt was an early edition of the newspaper, soaked with his blood. There was a half-smoked cigarette inside his shirt where it had dropped from his mouth when he was shot—once in the back and twice in the head with .45-calibre bullets.

Danny Brent's murder was the city's first gangland style execution in the fight for control over Vancouver's drug fiefdom, and it caused a sensation in the press. Headlines promising the "Inside Story" on Danny's murder and pictures showing police "probing clues" were splashed across the front pages of the dailies and provided true-crime grist for the Mickey Spillane fans of the time. There was an assortment of sketchy characters surrounding Brent—two ex-wives, rumours of a married girlfriend, and a Chicago-based drug syndicate. The plot wasn't bad either. There were the hired killers from out of town, the attempted murders of two other Vancouver drug lords, and a role for the chief of police, who would be kicked off the force the following year.

In 1954 Vancouver was filled with after-hours gambling joints, bootleggers thrived, and drugs were commonplace. The *Globe and Mail* reported that Vancouver had 2,000 known addicts and "scores of peddlers." The city's population was just under 400,000, and the police department was staffed with less than 700 working under Chief Walter Mulligan.

Danny Brent's Life of Crime

Drugs certainly weren't new to Vancouver; in fact, the city was known as "the drug capital of Canada." At the age of forty-two, Danny Brent was becoming a big part of the drug scene. On the day that he bled to death on the university golf course, he was also the head waiter at the Press Club at 595 Beatty Street and was vice-president of the Club, Cabaret, Culinary and Service Employees Union, Local No. 740.

People liked Danny, even his ex-wives. At the time of his death, he was renting a room from his first wife, Marie Brooks, on West 15th Avenue. He was hard-working and popular with both his employers and his colleagues. "He was a nice guy," a Press Club bartender told a reporter. "He could always talk a drunk out of the club. He never had to fight with them." Danny was also known to carry a big wad of money on him—usually between $2,000 and $3,000.

Danny was born in Edmonton, Alberta. His first stint behind bars was in 1929, when Danny, just seventeen, was caught stealing. He moved to BC and, after being caught for breaking and entering, spent another two years in a Kelowna, BC, jail before moving back to Alberta. In 1941, he and a colleague stole $50,000 worth of jewellery from Henry Birks and Sons; police found the stolen goods buried in the backyard of one of his relatives. Danny and his accomplice were convicted of receiving stolen property and sentenced to five years each. They appealed the conviction, and their sentences were increased to seven years. When he got out after serving the full seven-year sentence, Danny moved to Vancouver. Since then he'd managed to stay out of jail in Vancouver, just not out of trouble.

Danny worked at the Press Club at Dunsmuir and Beatty, just up the street from the Sun Tower. As its name suggests, the Press Club attracted members of the press, but also police and lawyers, and people like Vancouver coroner Glen McDonald, who would investigate Danny's cause of death. Tom Ardies, a *Vancouver Sun* reporter, described the art in the Club in one of his stories of that year: "You can wander into the Press Club where Brent was head waiter and worked beneath the bizarre murals. One shows a man slumped over a card table. There's a knife stuck in his back. There's a reporter snitching a pickle off the dead man's plate."

According to *Police Beat*, a book written in 1991 by Joe Swan, a former sergeant with the Vancouver Police Department, Danny dealt in brown heroin, which he bought in bulk from importers in Eastern Canada who, in turn, obtained their supplies from Mexico. He bundled the heroin up in fifty-capsule lots and employed a man to "plant" the bundles at the foot of various trees along English Bay. The man was paid twenty dollars for each planting, and Danny would then sell the location of each "plant" to street pushers.

Police Probe Clues in Brent Murder

On the night of his murder, Danny started his shift at the Press Club at 8:45 p.m. He worked until shortly before 1:00 a.m. and left carrying a copy of that morning's *News-Herald* with a nearly completed crossword puzzle.

Witnesses told police that after leaving the Press Club, Danny met up with a woman at the Mayling Supper Club, a Chinatown cabaret on the corner of Main and East Pender. He parked his car—a red 1950 Meteor convertible—in the parking lot at the back of the building. Another witness who was in the club that night told police that he had seen Danny leave with a woman and two other men through the back door. A few minutes after the four left the club, customers said they heard a loud bang coming from the parking lot. They told police that it sounded like a firecracker or a car backfiring and didn't bother to investigate.

Police believe that Danny slid behind the wheel of his car, lit up a cigarette, and was shot in the back by one of the men. The first bullet pierced his spine

Vancouver Sun, September 17, 1954

POLICE PROBE CLUES IN BRENT MURDER

Royal Canadian Mounted Police experts combed every inch of this car belonging to slain club waiter Danny Brent Thursday in order to find clues to killers who dumped victim's body on University golf course. Bloodstains and bits of grass were found on car and right front hubcap was missing.

Police search for evidence from Danny Brent's car.

at a downward angle and then tore a hole in his liver before it came out his navel. Dr T.R. Harmon, the pathologist, said he could have lived up to half an hour after this shot was fired.

From the tire tracks embedded in the golf course, investigators determined that the killers had driven onto the course from University Boulevard, down the fairway, and across to the west edge of the green. They dragged Danny out of the car, dumped him near some bushes, and shot him again, this time twice in the head. The second bullet was fired into his head from behind the right ear, and the third went through both cheeks.

The killers returned to the car and drove back the way they had come. Police found the flashy convertible the next day, abandoned in the 3500 block of West Eleventh Avenue, only about a dozen blocks from where Danny's body was found.

When Vancouver Coroner Glen McDonald arrived at the golf course that morning, he found city police, science bureau personnel, and investigators already at the scene. Once Danny's body was taken away, police started to search the area for evidence. Bobby, the RCMP tracker dog, was brought in from Surrey, BC to help.

Police found a copper-jacketed slug from a .45 automatic buried ten inches (25.4 cm) in the ground underneath the spot where Danny's head had been. The second slug was only two inches (five cm) deep, stopped by the thick sod. They found a piece of gold filling from his tooth embedded in the grass. Time of death was estimated to be between 2:00 and 3:00 a.m.

"This may see the start of an all-out gang war," McDonald told reporters.

Province reporter and photographer Ray Munro had received a tip about the body and arrived at the crime scene shortly after McDonald. He walked to the tenth hole, a short walk through the fog from the road. "Two detectives and three groundsmen were there, and so was Danny Brent—dead, with three bullet holes in his body, which was twisted up like a discarded rag doll," wrote Munro in *The Sky's No Limit*. "Whoever pulled the trigger wanted to leave a highly visible message that whatever Brent had done to deserve such an end would not be tolerated."

The killers made no effort to hide the body or disguise Danny's identity. Robbery was quickly ruled out. While there was only $2.05 in change in his pockets, he was still wearing an expensive wrist watch, a gold ring on the fourth finger of his right hand, and a gold band mounted with a black stone on the ring finger of his left hand.

Underworld Shaken by Brent's Killing

Four days after his murder, police opened a locker in the Vancouver Bus Depot and found thirty ounces (0.9 g) of heroin with a street value of $175,000. It was quickly apparent that there was more to Danny than head waiter and union official. Either he was killed by a gang trying to take over the heroin industry or, more likely, he was murdered by a hit team because he had reneged on a drug debt.

As detectives questioned dozens of drug dealers and addicts, a picture started to emerge of a struggle for control of the Vancouver drug trade. "Brent must have double-crossed a big boy. I believe it was a double-cross at the very top of Canada's drug trade," an anonymous police source told a *Vancouver Sun* reporter. "I believe the murder was done by imported hoodlums because the local boys wouldn't be trusted with such an assignment." But none of the suspects identified by the police department could be tied to Danny's murder.

One of reporter Munro's sources told him that he worked for Danny pushing heroin until two days before his death, and that Danny was second from the top in a drug wholesaling outfit that sold well-diluted heroin to distributors who cut it again and sold it to street pushers, who then doubled the amount by adding milk sugar and sold it to addicts.

Danny, wrote Munro, had been told to stop operating west of Granville Street—a north-south thoroughfare that effectively divided the city in two—by Jacob Leonhardt, who fronted for the branch of the Mafia that smuggled

Vancouver Sun, September 17, 1954

The Mayling Supper Club, far right, was the last place Danny Brent was seen alive.

the stuff into the city. Leonhardt claimed that territory as his own. According to Munro, Danny was also having serious problems with William Semenick, another major drug mover.

As investigators continued to run down leads, police had Danny's abandoned car towed back to the police garage, and police scientists spent several hours in a search for evidence. The folded newspaper stuffed inside Danny's shirt to stop his blood from getting on the car seat didn't do the job. There were blood stains in the car, and officers also found bits of grass from the golf course. A sign sat under the wipers reading "don't touch" until fingerprints could be processed, but in the end only Danny's fingerprints and blood were found.

Two days after the murder, RCMP officers were back scouring the crime scene with the help of a metal detector, hoping to find the murder weapon or any object accidentally dropped by the killers. But the gun that killed Danny Brent wouldn't be found for another twenty-four years.

Gangland Murder Thwarted in Stanley Park

On November 3, less than two months after Danny Brent's murder, the drug war heated up again with the attempted murder of William Semenick, a fifty-year-old career criminal. It was the second attempt on his life. The first had occurred in 1950 when killers slipped into the backyard of his home on West 10th Avenue and fired two shots at him through the kitchen window. Both missed.

Semenick had since separated from his wife, Dorothy, and their two small children and was living at the Buchan Hotel on Haro Street, where he was abducted around midnight and then driven to Stanley Park to be murdered. Semenick told police that while his kidnappers were driving through the West End, one with a gun against his ear, he managed to edge sideways until he got the door handle under his elbow. When the car slowed down near Lumberman's Arch in Stanley Park, Semenick pushed the door open and he and his would-be assassin fell out. As he ran from the car, one bullet ripped through his hat while the second hit him in the thigh. That would likely have been the end of Semenick, but for police constable Bill Lindsay who was making a routine drive through the park right at that moment. When Lindsay arrived on the scene, he heard the gun shots, saw a car speeding away without its lights, and a man plunge into the bush. Then he saw Semenick staggering toward him calling, "Help me, I'm shot."

Less than half an hour after the shooting, and with the help of an alert janitor from the nearby Vancouver Rowing Club, police found Eddie Sherban,

Vancouver Sun, November 4, 1954

FROGMAN RETRIEVES SHOOTING EVIDENCE

Amateur diver, Constable B. C. Maloney (in water), dived to bottom near the Rowing Club float Tuesday afternoon and came up with evidence believed dropped by one of suspects in Monday shooting in Stanley Park. Police refused to release any details as to what he found.—George Diack photo.

Constable Maloney dives to the bottom of the water near the Rowing Club to find a gun dropped by one of the suspects in the attempted murder of William Semenick in Stanley Park.

twenty-two, hiding neck deep in the waters of Coal Harbour and clutching the stern of the yacht *Marsel*. Later that day, police arrested Joseph Marcoux, twenty-eight, a former minor league hockey player from Manitoba. Both men were charged with attempted murder.

While Semenick was recovering in hospital from his gunshot wound, police charged him with another trafficking offence. He was convicted and sentenced to ten years in prison after being told by the judge that only his age and a recent heart attack saved him from the maximum fourteen-year term.

Semenick refused to identify his would-be murderers because he told police he wouldn't last long in jail if he did. His silence earned him the nickname "Silent Bill," and while it may have kept him alive, it cost him, too; another three months was tacked onto his sentence for his attempt to obstruct justice.

In another interesting twist at the trial, Constable Joseph Haywood, who had been on the police force for only a year, was tasked with guarding Semenick while he was in hospital. The twenty-seven-year-old constable took an off-duty job moonlighting as a driver and bodyguard for Semenick without informing his superiors, and later testified in court that he was gathering evidence in his "undercover" role. Semenick fought Haywood's evidence, claiming that the rookie officer had only become an "undercover agent" after he was caught being a criminal.

Car Bomb Blast Rocks District: Victim Guarded in Hospital

Shortly after Semenick was safely tucked away in jail, Jacob Leonhardt, a leader of another faction of Vancouver's drug world, was almost killed when a home-made bomb with dynamite wired to the ignition shredded his expensive Buick in the driveway of his home at Heather Street and 41st Avenue.

The explosion, which was felt nearly a mile (1.6 km) away, blew out the windows of Leonhardt's home and that of his neighbours. The car's hood was found in the backyard of a neighbour; it had been blasted right over Leonhardt's garage. A front fender, a rear door, and a seat were strewn in a line to the left of the car. The sliding doors of the garage were blown off, part of the roof was shattered, and there was broken glass everywhere. Leonhardt, thirty-eight, was thrown ten feet (three metres) by the blast and lost a leg in the explosion.

Police found a rifle with a telescopic sight in the back of his mangled car. Neighbours told reporters that Jacob and Pauline had two children, a baby called Jack, and a seven-year-old girl named Sharon. The Leonhardts had lived in the house for two years, but the neighbours were unsure what he did for a living. One said he thought Jacob was a carpenter, another a taxi driver. Leonhardt was listed in the city directory of that year as a car salesman.

Later that year, Leonhardt tried to sue the *Vancouver Sun* for libel. The judge awarded him one dollar in damages saying that, "In my estimation the Plaintiff has no reputation capable of being injured." Newspapers reported that he was also having trouble collecting from his insurance company.

No one was ever charged with the attempted murder of Jacob Leonhardt.

All-Out War on Drugs Ordered in Vancouver

By the end of 1954, Vancouver police were dealing with seven murders, the highest count since 1948—and this didn't include Danny Brent, who was murdered outside the city's boundaries.

"We're going all out to crack down on this crime wave," Mayor Fred Hume told reporters in December 1954. "If the thugs want to get tough, we can get tough too." Chief Constable Mulligan announced the formation of a twelve-man flying squad that would target drug addicts.

At the same time that it was reported that Vancouver had the highest rate of drug addiction in Canada, the city was also experiencing a drug shortage brought about by irregular supplies of heroin at street level as the rival factions fought to gain control of the drug world. As the shortage pushed up prices, addicts turned to crime or ramped up their criminal activities to feed their habits. In a six-week period over November and December of 1954, the *Globe and Mail* reported that the Greater Vancouver area was hit by eight armed bank robberies netting more than $100,000, while sixty-six small retail stores were also robbed.

The unsolved murder of Danny Brent and the ensuing attacks on Semenick and Leonhardt reflected badly on Chief Constable Walter Mulligan and his administration and helped to hasten his departure. In March 1955 Mulligan testified before a senate committee in Ottawa that was probing the drug situation in Canada. The twenty-three member committee visited Vancouver and said that the lack of enforcement was "wholly responsible" for the city's mounting drug problems. Senator Reid's report stated: "Where law enforcement is lax, that's where you find the big traffic in dope. In narcotics, Vancouver is Canada's capital."

By June of that year, Mulligan had a front seat at the Tupper Royal Commission into police corruption. It turned out that the chief of police was allowing the gambling squad to top up their paycheques with payoffs from criminals in return for turning a blind eye to the dozens of bookies and bootleggers operating illegal premises in Vancouver; Mulligan was pocketing half of the proceeds. Midway through the proceedings, Mulligan grabbed his wife Violet and skipped town. He became a limo dispatcher in California.

In 1962, following his early release from prison, Semenick moved to Victoria, BC. He gave an interview to a television reporter and told him that he was through with his life of crime. Semenick told the reporter that Canada's drug trafficking was controlled from New York through Toronto. He said Danny Brent was killed because he refused to pay for drugs.

According to his death certificate, Semenick died of a heart attack in 1970; he was sixty-six. His profession was listed as carpenter in the construction industry. Jacob Leonhardt died from a heart attack two years later. He was fifty-five.

Murder Case Revived as Rusty Gun Found

In 1975 a homeowner raking under a hedge near his home in the 3100 block on West 11th Avenue found a rusted .45-calibre automatic. He gave the gun to a friend who owned a gun shop on West 4th Avenue. The friend worked on the gun for a while then gave it up as a bad job and hung the weapon on a peg in the shop. There it stayed for another three years, until a sharp-eyed police officer saw it and had it seized.

The gun was found just a few blocks from where Danny Brent's car was abandoned after he was murdered more than twenty years earlier. While lab tests failed to prove that the rusty pistol was the murder weapon, ammunition found in the clip matched the make of the ammunition used to kill Danny. The gun was also found close to where a search had been abandoned following the murder. While pictures of the gun made a nice addition to the cold case files, Danny's murder remains unsolved.

Sources:
Globe and Mail: January 28, April 23, May 11, 1955; June 9, 1956; October 9, 1962; March 27, 1978
Province: November 3, 1954
Vancouver News-Herald: November 5, 16, 1954; February 16, 18; April 28, 1955
Vancouver Sun: September 15, 16, 17, 21; November 4, 1954; April 20, 1981

*"Mayor Fred Hume promised that the full power of the police
will be mobilized today to stamp out the mounting crime wave
turning Vancouver into a 'Little Chicago' with bizarre killings
and daring bank and drug store holdups."*
—Vancouver Sun, *November 9, 1954*

CHAPTER 5

Printer Strangled, Shot in Own Home

T he dust had barely settled on Danny Brent's unsolved murder file when a
new case shot to the front page of the dailies.

Robert David Hopkins, a forty-eight-year-old printer with the *Vancouver
News-Herald*, was found strangled and shot in the head in his quiet suburban
home. Sometime in the early hours of November 6, 1954, Robert Hopkins became
Vancouver's seventh murder victim, and his own newspaper's headline story.

From all accounts, Robert Hopkins lived a quiet life. The Irish-born bachelor
owned a neat little grey cottage in the Kensington-Cedar Cottage area of
Vancouver. Friends and neighbours described him as a mild, friendly man who
kept to himself and spent long hours in his garden.

Robert was gay, and like most homosexual men in the 1950s, he led a secret
life—straight at work, and gay in his social life. While the media hinted at his
homosexuality, nothing overt was ever printed in the newspapers of the day or
voiced aloud by his neighbours and friends. Homosexuals simply didn't exist.

Vancouver News-Herald, November 9, 1954

Robert Hopkins
was murdered
in his house on
Fleming Street in
November 1954.

There were three daily newspapers operating in Vancouver in 1954—the *Vancouver Sun*, the *Province*, and the *Vancouver News-Herald*. The latter was founded in 1933, with a circulation of 10,000. Always the underdog, it was a feisty paper, well laid-out, and staffed with well-known newspaper people such as Pierre Berton, the paper's city editor when he was just twenty-one, Barry Broadfoot, and Himie Koshevoy, who became managing editor at the *Vancouver Sun*. In those early years, reporters sat on orange crates and shared typewriters. The September before Robert was murdered, the paper shortened its name to the *Herald* and moved into a larger building on West Georgia (where the luxury hotel and condo tower known as the Shangri-La Vancouver now sits). At the time of Robert Hopkin's death, the *Herald* called itself "Western Canada's Largest Morning Herald." And because it was a morning paper, the *Herald* was scooped by its competitors on its own employee's murder.

He Was a Quiet Man

When the *Herald* did run a catch-up story on its front page the next day, it had photographs of Robert's cottage as well as one showing a smiling, balding man wearing small round glasses. Robert had his portrait taken at Marlow's of British Columbia Ltd, a studio at Dunsmuir and Seymour streets that specialized in fashion and society photos. When he picked up two sets of the photos shortly before his death, he told owner Reuben Marlow that one was for his sister May, a school teacher in Edmonton, and the other he'd had taken for a "special friend." Marlow told reporters that Robert appeared to be in a "happy frame of mind ... He was a very peaceful and friendly person," he said.

Robert was born in Belfast, Ireland, and moved to Edmonton with his parents as a small child. He apprenticed as a printer, moved to Vancouver in 1947, and spent a couple of years working at Union Printers before moving over to the composing room at the *Vancouver News-Herald*. His closest relative was his sister May. Another sister, who lived in Vancouver, had died of a heart attack a few months before he was murdered.

Robert didn't turn up for his Friday night shift. And when he failed to turn up for his Sunday night shift at the *Herald* and had not called in, his co-workers became worried. George Jones, foreman of the composing room, and Ernest Whitehouse, a printer who knew Robert from Edmonton, called around to his house when their shift ended shortly after midnight. Jones and Whitehouse found all the doors locked, the blinds drawn, and Friday afternoon's and Saturday morning's newspapers still on the front porch. When repeated knocking on both front and back doors didn't elicit a response, Jones and Whitehouse went in search of a policeman.

Jones waved down a passing police cruiser. The officer came back with them to the house, and called his duty sergeant. When the sergeant arrived, he went to the back of the house and dragged a ladder out of the basement. "We held it against the side of the house while the sergeant went up it and into a window. The first thing he said when he got the window open and the blind up was, 'There he is. He's inside all right,'" Jones told the reporter.

Even for a veteran police officer, the murder scene was horrific. Robert Hopkins lay face up on the floor of his living room in front of the sofa. He was dressed in T-shirt, pants, shoes, and socks. An electric light cord was wrapped around his neck and two pillows were placed over his face. When the officer removed the pillows, he saw that Robert's face was covered in blood and that there was a hole in his head. His feet were tied with a necktie, and his pants had been pulled down. A pair of scissors and a penny lay beside his feet.

The house was a shambles. Drawers and cupboards were ransacked and their contents scattered everywhere. Furniture lay strewn about, giving the impression that Robert had put up a fight.

The coroner determined that he had been strangled and then shot with a .22-calibre gun sometime on the Friday night or in the early hours of Saturday morning.

Motive a Mystery

The most obvious motive was robbery, especially when police were unable to find either a wallet or money in the house. Also missing was a black leather Gladstone bag, a gold pocket watch engraved with the dead man's initials, and a pair of Japanese binoculars in a case. These items were never recovered.

Robert Hopkins was comfortably well-off. He earned $100 a week from his job at the *Herald* and had close to $10,000 in savings. The extraordinarily brutal method of killing seemed extreme for a robbery or home invasion, and police moved on to other theories. Because of the recent spate of shootings—Danny Brent's murder the previous September and the attempted murder of William Semenick in Stanley Park just days before—police searched for a connection. Danny's job as a bartender at the Press Club certainly would have introduced him to staff from all three daily newspapers. Between 1951 and 1966, the Press Club had a gay piano player appearing six nights a week, and while it was essentially "straight," gays were tolerated. But even in a semi-tolerant environment, it's unlikely Robert would have wanted anyone to connect his work world with his homosexuality.

Ron Dutton, archivist for the BC Gay and Lesbian Archives, notes that in 1954, most gay people would have hidden their sexuality. "To be out was to be ostracized socially. You'd lose your job, you'd lose your family, you'd lose your place in the community, and you would be identified as an easy target for violence," he says. "So many gay people lived permanently closeted lives."

Frustrated by the lack of leads, reporters interviewed Robert's co-workers and neighbours in an effort to find a new motive for his murder. But no one seemed to know him very well, and colleagues described him as a good worker who led a quiet life. One co-worker told a reporter: "He was the kind of a man you could work beside for years and never really get to know him." Another said: "He was not the kind that would have a beer or sit in [on] a poker game."

"I can't understand it," said Doug Milne, another *Herald* printer. "I didn't know him too well, but we had gone to Theatre Under the Stars together a few times, and I had visited his home afterward. Even when he took a drink, he wasn't belligerent. After a couple of drinks, he would fall asleep in his chair." Ernest Whitehouse, one of the men who found his body and knew him in Edmonton, said: "He is about the last man in the world you would expect to die violently. To the best of my knowledge, he didn't have an enemy in the world." Robert had lived at 4010 Fleming Street in East Vancouver for about five years, and his neighbours also described him as a quiet man who kept his home clean and neat and had quiet, conservative habits.

"The last time I saw Mr Hopkins was on Thursday when he walked past the house and waved to me in the window," said Mary Weir, who lived a few doors down. "He brought me three lovely roses a week ago last Sunday."

Louise Laviolette, his next-door neighbour, said, "He was such a nice quiet man and never bothered anyone. Sometimes he would bring a friend or two home for a drink, but he never held any noisy parties. Only once can I remember any incident and that was only a few people singing. He was wonderful to the children and was always giving them candy."

Neighbours said he was known to have friends drop by, but "none of them are believed to have been women."

Dark-Haired Mystery Man

While the newspapers avoided any outright reference to homosexuality, the police investigation seemed to be heading in that direction.

Herald employees told police that Robert had been seen in the company of a dark-haired "mystery man," and they'd met several times in recent weeks. The mystery man was apparently unemployed, and they said that Robert had loaned him money. One employee said that he had given Robert and this friend a ride to Robert's home on a couple of occasions.

Police refused to say how Robert's murderers got into the house, whether they forced their way inside or were admitted by him.

An article in the *West Ender* written in 1984 by Joe Swan, a former Vancouver police officer, sheds a little more light on the original police investigation. Swan writes that Robert was known to occasionally meet men after his work shift and would sometimes take them to his home for a drink. "The police investigation commenced, as is usual, with a thorough check of all the people who had known, worked, or had any past dealings with the victim," Swan writes. "In this instance their job was made easier because Hopkins had kept an address book in which he wrote the addresses of even those casual acquaintances he had met and invited to his home."

There were few places for gay men to safely meet other gay men in the 1950s—at private house parties, skid row bars, or illegal booze cans that catered to the gay community. The BC Gay and Lesbian Archives files have several accounts from men who spoke about the gay scene in Vancouver in the 1950s. One mentions "G," the chauffeur for one of Vancouver's wealthiest families, who threw wild parties for gay policemen in the gatehouse of a South Granville estate.

A 1994 issue of *The Peak* gives a first-hand account of being gay in post-war Vancouver: "Thank God for the Hotel Vancouver! It had a beer parlour in the basement with two sections, 'ladies and escorts' and 'men.' The men's side was strictly gay. It was small, I forget what the seating capacity of it was, it couldn't be more than fifty or sixty. If you weren't in by six on Friday or Saturday you just didn't get a seat."

There were a handful of nightclubs and hotels where gay men could congregate, such as the Castle Hotel at 750 Granville Street. The Montreal Club was an after-hours BYOB club on Main and Hastings where gay men could dance together. While these nightclubs and hotels gave homosexuals a place to meet, it was by no means safe, says BC Gay and Lesbian archivist Ron Dutton.

When he started to research violence against gay men in the 1950s, Dutton was surprised at the extreme brutality of the assaults. "There was a great danger of being murdered and a high degree of social acceptance toward violence against gay people," says Dutton. "Somehow they deserved this, so the authorities looked the other way and they wouldn't investigate very hard. It would be very hard to make a conviction."

Dutton says that if a crime against a gay person did make it to court, the

Courtesy Vancouver Archives CVA780-57

The Castle Hotel on Granville Street, pictured here in 1965, was a well-known gay hang-out.

"homosexual panic defense" was standard fare for lawyers until the 1980s and was highly successful in beating the charge. In this defense, the defendant claims that he was the object of a sexual advance by a homosexual and the defendant found the advance so offensive and frightening that he had to retaliate with unusual force and violence. "At every step through the criminal justice system, gay people knew how vulnerable they were and consequently were deeply in the closet around their sexual identities," says Dutton.

Dutton has a thin file of articles on the Robert Hopkins murder. He notes that it was common for the media to report on a murder or act of violence and filter out gay content. "The 'legitimate media' wouldn't touch any gay subject," he says. "Being gay was illegal, it was immoral, and it was thought of as a mental illness, and that lasted right up into the '60s." If gays or lesbians were mentioned at all in the 1950s, it was as "perverts," "deviates," or "inverts," or else they were lumped together with pedophiles and rapists under the general term of "sexual deviancy." In fact, homosexuality wasn't decriminalized in Canada until 1969 as a result of legislation introduced two years earlier.

The final story to appear about Robert Hopkins' murder in the *Herald* ran following his autopsy, eleven days after his death. After determining cause of death was a gunshot wound to the forehead, the headline was: "Herald Man's Death Ruled Unnatural."

Sources:
Globe and Mail: November 10, 1954   *Vancouver Sun*: November 8, 9, 1954
Province: November 8, 9, 1954   *The Peak*: May 1994
Vancouver News-Herald: November 9, 1954   *The West Ender*: September 6, 1984

"Sexually unbalanced males are found now in increasing numbers and out of proportion to the increase of the city's population," said Chief Constable George Archer in 1958. "We are now dealing with the most dangerous form of sex deviation, which involves personal attack."

CHAPTER 6

The Hastings-Sunrise Murder

Vancouver of the 1950s was still a small town in many respects. People didn't lock their doors, and they knew their neighbours. It was the decade of the first Corvette and the '57 Chevy, and because television was still a novelty, people were staying home on Saturday nights to watch *Father Knows Best, Leave It to Beaver, Hockey Night in Canada,* or *Front Page Challenge.*

But the city also had a nasty undercurrent, especially toward women who had been given a taste of independence and access to decent jobs during the war years. Domestic violence was largely ignored and women still had few rights. Children had fewer. "Certainly in the '50s it was totally permissible for mothers and fathers to whack their children in the grocery store. Teachers would hit children, and the notion that a man could 'correct' his spouse was seen as totally acceptable," says Neil Boyd, Director of the School of Criminology at Simon Fraser University.

Early in the decade, a man dubbed "the love bandit" by the press had terrorized women in Vancouver for four years by stalking them, cutting their telephone wires, breaking into their homes, and kissing them. By the time the ex-policeman was caught, he had attacked thirty women.

In 1955, the first year that the Vancouver Police Department recorded sexual assaults separately in the annual report, seventeen rapes were reported, and seven men were arrested and charged. The following year, there were twenty-five rapes reported and another seven were attempted.

Between December 1957 and February 1959, a man known as the Point Grey Molester broke into the bedrooms of seventeen women in the middle of the night, shone a flashlight into their faces, and while threatening the women with a sheath knife, forced them to strip. While he never raped them, he made them perform various sexual acts. The women described him as "young and inexperienced," and part of his signature was to unscrew the light bulb and plunge the room into darkness. Barry McLintock neglected to wear gloves and was eventually arrested after police lifted fingerprints from a bulb and scored a hit when the youth was caught robbing a bus driver.

But it wasn't until the murder of Evelyn Roche on April 3, 1958 that the women of Vancouver really knew true fear.

Police Hunt Fiend in City Murder

Chief Constable George Archer warned the city that "a sex fiend" was on the loose, that he believed that he would murder again, and that women should travel in pairs or be met by a male escort if they were coming home after dark. The Chief said that violent sexual attacks against women had shown up in three separate areas around Vancouver, and in attempting to cope with this violence, some police had been redeployed from their "normal" duties to the extent where citizens' lives were endangered. "No further deployment can be made," he said.

To women who might be at risk for being molested at night, and who presumably couldn't count on more police presence, the chief advised, "Scream. Scream immediately, loud and long, that's the best defence."

All of this was little comfort to the family of Evelyn Roche. Evelyn was born in Nelson, BC, and moved to Vancouver in the early 1940s. Her husband died in a construction-site accident, leaving her to raise their two children, Sharon and Frank. Evelyn was a hairdresser by trade and entrepreneurial by nature. The family lived near Hornby and Davie streets in downtown Vancouver, and Evelyn and her best friend Helen Olson ran a small café nearby.

Courtesy Sharon Harder

Evelyn Roche at the Dumaresq logging camp at Seymour Inlet, September 1957.

Sharon and Frank on Hornby Street, where Evelyn and Helen Olson ran a small café, ca. 1947.

Evelyn's daughter Sharon now says it was a sketchy area at the time. She remembers one character they just called "Red" because of his red hair, but she later found out that his real name was Frederick Ducharme, and he was a particular nasty piece of work. Ducharme was convicted of murdering Blanche Fisher, a forty-five-year-old dress-fitter at Woodward's Department Store, in 1949. He was hanged the following year.

Evelyn and Helen sold the café and opened a variety store on Oak Street, and the women bought a rooming house on Commercial Drive and East 11th Avenue. They rented rooms to friends, and Evelyn had taken pity on an old man who had been gassed in the Boer War, set him up in a room, and used to cook for him. "She was a wonderful person," recalls her son Frank. "And she was a hell of a good cook. She could look in the fridge and there'd be nothing there and somehow she'd come up with a stew or a hash." Adds Sharon: "Everybody loved her. She had such a good sense of humour; she was very, very funny, and she always kept herself looking very nice."

Evelyn and Helen both got jobs cooking at a logging camp where they'd work ten days at the camp and were home for five. They hired a housekeeper to take care of the children while they were away. It was at the camp where Evelyn met logger Richard Roche. They married in 1955.

Courtesy Sharon Harder

Evelyn and Helen on the boat at the Whonnock logging camp.

Courtesy Sharon Harder

Evelyn and Richard Roche at the Mayling Cabaret, ca. 1957.

"We just adored him; he was so good for us, a lot of fun," says Sharon. "They were just so good together, so compatible."

Evelyn and the kids would join Richard at the logging camp during their holidays, and Sharon remembers how much her mother loved to fish and enjoyed the lifestyle. "I think if we'd been out of school, she would have moved into the logging camp with my dad," says Sharon.

In 1958 Evelyn and Richard decided to buy a place of their own in the Hastings-Sunrise neighbourhood of Vancouver. Sharon was sixteen, Frank fourteen. "It was just up from Vancouver Tech, where we went to school, and it was a really lovely house," says Sharon. "My mum was just thrilled. It was so fancy compared to what we had before." After the family moved in a few days before Easter, Richard left for the Dumaresq Logging Company, located at Seymour Inlet about 210 miles (340 km) north of Vancouver.

On the night before Good Friday, the Roches' realtor dropped by with some papers to sign, and they had a celebratory drink to toast the new house. Since Richard couldn't come home for Easter, Evelyn decided to take the bus to the liquor store downtown where she could send him a bottle of Irish whiskey. She asked the kids to go with her, but they wanted to watch a television show called *Oh! Susanna* and declined. Sharon's last words to her mother were, "Mum, please don't forget the grapes."

Eve Lazarus photo, 2014

The Roches moved into their house on East 6th just a few days before Evelyn was murdered.

Evelyn was an attractive thirty-nine-year-old woman who stood five feet, six inches tall, had brown eyes, dark brown hair, and a Roman nose. That night, she was smartly dressed in a skirt matched with a blue and green blouse and green sweater and black high-heeled shoes. Because it was cold, she put on her navy blue coat and red gloves.

Evelyn left the house at 8:00 p.m. and caught the bus to Commercial Drive, stopping at Louie's grocery store to buy grapes. She transferred to a downtown bus, went to the liquor store on West Pender Street where she bought a bottle of whiskey and had it sent to Richard, and bought another to take home. A bus driver who recognized her picture told police that she left his bus at Broadway and Penticton streets around 10:20 p.m. The driver remembered a man also getting off at that stop.

Detectives believe that Evelyn was walking down Penticton when she was grabbed and dragged into a lane just two blocks from her house.

Killer Punched, Stabbed

Albert Jeal was crossing Penticton at East 7th Avenue around 10:30 p.m. when he heard a woman's scream coming from the lane. He glanced in the direction of the scream, decided it was just teenagers, and ignored it. "The screams," he said, "were spaced close together, just long enough in between for a person to draw breath."

Courtesy Sharon Harder

Evelyn tending to her garden.

Don Varner, who lived close to where Evelyn's body was found, told police that a noise woke him about 11:00 p.m. "These moaning sounds were about two or three minutes apart," he told a reporter. "I looked out the back window, saw nothing, and went back to sleep."

Varner's son, nineteen-year-old Bobby, said he drove home around 11:00 p.m. and saw "a woman, her face all bloodied," in the lane. He didn't get out of the car because he thought she had been beaten up and her assailant might still be around, so he drove off to find police. By the time he returned home to phone police, they had already been called by John McKenna.

McKenna, a Canadian National Railway employee, had just left his house and was walking up to Broadway to meet a friend who drove him to work. There was a full moon that night, and as he glanced down the lane he saw Evelyn's body. "I didn't know what was wrong with her, so when I met my driver at Penticton and Broadway, we came back and took a flashlight into the lane," he said. "We walked to within about thirty feet [9.1 m] of her then decided we'd better not go any further because it looked bad, and we didn't want to mess anything up for the police."

Evelyn had been stabbed in the neck, chest, and back, each wound delivered with such force that the blade had entered her body to the hilt. She had been dragged by the legs, and her underwear was ripped and smeared with blood.

There were blood stains around each ankle. Two brown paper bags were found near her body. One contained the grapes, the other a bottle of Canadian Club Rye with a receipt from the liquor store on West Pender Street.

At daylight the next morning, police searched the lanes, ditches, garbage cans, and yards in the area trying to find either the murder weapon, a purse, or some identification. Other police went from door to door to find out if anyone had seen or heard anything that could help the investigation. Because there was no identification on Evelyn's body, police gave a full description to the radio stations.

"She didn't come home, and I was up all night. I had this awful, awful feeling," says Sharon. "Then I heard on the radio that a body had been found, and I phoned the police station, and I said, 'I think that's my mum.'"

Sharon phoned Helen Olson, and at 9:00 a.m. on Good Friday, Helen went to the morgue and identified the body of her best friend.

Slayer Returned to Scene

Several hours later that day, ten-year-old Peter Brookfield was visiting the Varners with his family and started to explore the neighbourhood. He found Evelyn's black cloth purse in a garbage can a block away from the murder site. Inside was twenty-seven dollars, her identification, and a hanky.

Because all the garbage cans had already been thoroughly searched, police believed that the killer lived in the area and had dumped the purse in the garbage as he passed by it sometime that day. They began a background check into all males living within a ten-block radius of the murder.

Robbery was quickly ruled out, and while Evelyn had not been raped, police determined that the assault was sexually motivated. "We believe there was a man looking for a woman, any woman, and the victim happened to come along. She resisted, and the killer stabbed her," police told reporters. "Having gone over the line and afraid of the consequences, he continued stabbing her in a frenzy." The killer, police told reporters, must have had been covered in blood, and someone must have seen him.

At around 8:00 a.m. on Saturday, April 5, eight blocks from where Evelyn was murdered and just two days later, a man wielding a knife threatened a forty-two-year-old woman at Broadway and Commercial Drive. She told police he was between twenty-five and thirty, five-foot-ten, 150 pounds (68 kg), with a fair complexion, and wearing a blue jacket and brown pants. She said he stopped her and showed her a stag-handle knife, which he held in one hand while rubbing the blade in "a threatening manner" with his other hand.

It was the only lead police had, and while three men were taken in for questioning, including the owner of a light blue and white car similar to one reported to have been cruising the murder area on Thursday night, none were arrested.

By the end of the year, police had drawn a blank.

"Every known sex offender in the city and surrounding areas has been questioned, and the questioning of residents in the area has been pursued endlessly," wrote Chief Archer in the 1958 police department annual report. "Hundreds of letters have been followed up for the slightest clue but, at the time of this report, no one has been connected with this crime. The case is still an open file, and work is continuing, running down leads and interviewing persons."

Not only did Frank and Sharon lose their mother, they were hounded by media and the public. Jack Webster, a well-known radio personality, emphasized her drinking and suggested that she was out gallivanting—that, in some way, the murder was her own fault.

"She was just doing my dad a favour," says Frank. "They were head-over-heels in love with each other."

Reporters hounded the family. "They would sit outside our house and try to take our pictures," says Sharon. "People would drive by our house."

Evelyn and Richard Roche enjoying a night out with friends, ca. 1957.

Courtesy Sharon Harder

Shortly after his wife's murder, Richard adopted Frank and Sharon. He kept the family in the house and hired a housekeeper to take care of the kids while he was away at work. Frank eventually joined his father as a logger, and Sharon married in 1961.

In 1985 after a story appeared about Evelyn's murder in the *West Ender*, a resident of the 2600 block East 8th Avenue told police that he had found a rusted switchblade with a bone handle on the overhang of his rear garage roof. The knife had only minor weathering due to exposure, but it could not be determined if it was the actual murder weapon.

"I've thought about this for years," says Frank. "I still don't know what happened that night. Why did this guy do that? It was obviously premeditated. He's walking around with a knife, and he is going to attack somebody. It wasn't robbery. My mum was in the wrong place at the wrong time."

Evelyn's case has not been reinvestigated, to Sharon and Frank's knowledge. But in 2008—fifty years after their mother's murder—Sharon received a phone call from the Vancouver Police Department. They told her that they wanted to return her mother's wedding ring, found on her body the night of her death, and the bottle of Irish whiskey.

Sources:
Vancouver Sun: April 5, 7, 8, 1958
Province: April 5, 9, 1958
West Ender: February 28; June 27, 1985
Globe and Mail: July 18, 1951

"The usually quiet, peaceful neighbourhood was thrown into fear
as soon as the grim story inside the brown stucco house was known.
Mothers herded their small daughters off the street into their homes.
Some took their children right out of the neighbourhood for the night."
—Vancouver Sun, *June 12, 1958*

CHAPTER 7

Vancouver's First Triple Murder

On June 10, 1958, Constables Bob Eagle and Russell Reid pulled up outside the Pauls' bungalow at 1014 East 53rd Avenue. The first thing they noticed was the pile of advertising flyers on the porch. Reid, the junior partner with just two years on the job, pounded on the door, and when no one answered he walked around the back. He found the porch door unlocked. Reid opened it and knocked on the inside door.

"I turned the knob and it opened, and I can still tell you what I said: 'Yoo-hoo, is anybody home'?" The unfortunate twenty-three-year-old Constable Reid was about to discover Vancouver's first triple murder involving two adults and their eleven-year-old daughter.

The Pauls' house on East 53rd Avenue in 1958.

As he walked through the house, Reid noticed a woman's purse lying open with the contents spread across the kitchen table. He entered the hallway and saw Helen Pauls lying face down, shards of glass from her smashed glasses scattered around her face, and blood spread out in front of her and around her head. She was wearing a dress, short coat, and shoes.

"I bent down and touched her leg. I probably shouldn't have, but I did, and it was cold," says Reid. "I called to my partner—'Bob, you should see what we've got here'—and he must have heard the quivering in my voice because he said, 'Let me in!' I opened the door, and he had his revolver out and we searched the house."

The horrified officers proceeded along the hallway. They found a young girl's body on the bed, wearing only the top half of her pyjamas, with her left leg stretched out to the floor. Reid couldn't help but notice that the little girl's school clothes were neatly laid out, ready for the following day.

The officers took the stairs down into the basement. There was so much blood on the floor upstairs that it was dripping through the ceiling and onto the mat below, said Reid. As they entered the basement, the officers saw the fully dressed body of fifty-three-year-old David Pauls lying in a pool of congealed blood in the otherwise neat and tidy room.

Constable Reid said the murders have haunted him for years. In those days, there were no grief counsellors, and he was traumatized by the scene and plagued with nightmares.

Chief Fears Fiend Will Murder Again

The city was still reeling from Evelyn Roche's murder two months before. Newspaper stories ran with headlines that proclaimed "Chief Fears Fiend Will Murder Again," and Chief George Archer held press conferences warning women to "travel in pairs" or arrange to be met by a male escort.

Forty-five-year-old Helen Pauls worked the 3:00 to 11:00 p.m. shift at the Home Fancy Sausage Shop, a Russian-owned deli on East Hastings Street. She took the bus home after work and usually arrived there at 11:30 p.m., but every night since Evelyn's murder, David Pauls drove to the bus stop at Fraser Street and 53rd Avenue to pick up his wife.

And then one night, he wasn't there. Shortly before midnight, Helen's neighbour saw her running down the street trying to stay dry by holding a newspaper over her head. David Pauls was most likely already dead.

The neighbour's sighting of Helen gave the police a timeline to go on. Because there was no forced entry, investigators believed that David had left the house by the side door to pick up Helen as he always did. It was raining hard that night, visibility was poor, and David was carrying a flashlight, which was later found in the grass in the backyard along with some of his blood.

Most likely David was crossing the backyard to where he kept their old pickup truck and surprised a trespasser—a peeping Tom, a robber, even a Russian hitman—and then was forced at gunpoint to return to the house. A large pool of congealed blood found on the rear steps of the house indicated that he had been shot there in the back of the head, struck twice with a heavy object, and then shot twice more at close range in the right temple. The killer dragged the 155-pound (70.3 kg) dead weight of David's body from the back steps of the house, inside and down the stairs to the basement. The killer took a lace from a pair of David's shoes, which were later found in a corner of the basement, and tied it around one of his wrists.

The rain would have muffled the sound of the gunshots so that the neighbours might not notice, but police believe that the noise woke Dorothy. The little girl was sitting up in bed when the killer made his way along the hallway to her bedroom. He smashed her head in with one blow.

Dorothy was found with a comforter wrapped around her head. The killer had pulled off her pajama bottoms, but she was not sexually assaulted. Police believe he may have been interrupted by her mother. Helen let herself in the front door, threw her purse on the kitchen table, and headed up the hallway to Dorothy's room. The killer stepped out and shot her in the face. The bullet

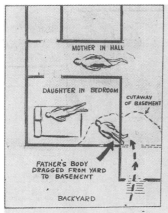

Vancouver Sun, June 12, 1958

POLICE, CROWDS SWARM OVER SCENE OF BRUTAL TRIPLE MURDER

GRISLY SCENE of triple murder of Mr. and Mrs. David Pauls and their daughter is shown in this artist's sketch. The parents had been beaten and shot to death and their daughter bludgeoned in her bed.

MOST BRUTAL MURDER in past 33 years in Vancouver is way veteran homicide officers describe slaying of the Pauls family. Body of one of the victims is taken from neat South Vancouver

house after city coroner Glen McDonald (on the porch) had surveyed grim scene. Death of family is estimated to have occurred about midnight Tuesday.—John Askew photo.

Left: Map of the house where the bodies were found. Right: Veteran homicide officers described the murders as the most brutal they'd seen. The body of one of the victims is taken from the South Vancouver house after city coroner Glen McDonald (on the porch) had surveyed the scene.

travelled through the lens of her glasses and into her right eye. She fell to the floor, and he shot her again in the side of her head. He then began to beat her. Afterward, he left the same way he came. As he cut across the yard, he dislodged a rock near the garage.

The murders shocked the city. People wondered how anything this brutal could happen to what seemed like such an ordinary, working-class family in their own home.

"House of Mystery For Years," Neighbours Say of Pauls' Home

At the time of their murders, David Pauls was a janitor with Woodward's Department Store, and Helen had worked at the Home Fancy Sausage Shop for the previous three years. Dorothy went to Walter Moberly Elementary School and had a tabby cat named Tiger. The Pauls owned a 1940s-style, grey stucco bungalow; Helen loved to garden, and the yard was always neatly trimmed and bright with flowers. High shrubs that surrounded the property hid the chicken coop from view and gave the house privacy and an air of mystery.

No one knew much about the Pauls, and that wasn't surprising. They both had full-time jobs and spent most of their weekends in the Fraser Valley. Helen's boss described her as a devout Mennonite who didn't drink, smoke, or wear lipstick. People remembered the Pauls as a hard-working, frugal couple who had no enemies. "They were very nice people, and there was no drinking. They never bothered anyone," a neighbour told a reporter after their murders.

Both David and Helen were born in Russia of Danish descent and grew up in German-speaking Mennonite families. David came to Canada in 1923 and worked as a farmhand at the Funk family's dairy farm in Hague, Saskatchewan. He married

Source: Vancouver Sun, June 12, 1958

Left: Neighbours tell police that they saw a "crazy" man behind the Pauls' house on the Saturday night before the murders. Centre: Dorothy's pet cat Tiger with Detective Bill Scott. Right: An abandoned car found three blocks from the Pauls' house is dusted for fingerprints by Constable Jack Murphy.

Helen, the Funks' youngest daughter, and one of ten children. After Helen died in childbirth in 1930 when she was just twenty-three years old, David bought a small farm in the Mennonite community and worked there for another ten years. His second wife was also named Helen. He married Helen Koop in 1940, and they moved to the Fraser Valley, probably to be closer to David's family. His mother, father, and brother Henry lived in Abbotsford. Another brother, George, lived in Kelowna. David also stayed close to the Funk family, and several of his former in-laws also moved to the Fraser Valley.

For a time, David worked at a sawmill, and in 1953 the family moved to Vancouver. City directories show that they lived first on Sophia Street and then on East 44th Avenue with another Mennonite family. The Pauls bought the house on East 53rd Avenue eighteen months before they were murdered.

South Vancouver of the 1950s had a very different demographic than it does today. There was a large Mennonite Brethren Church at 43rd Avenue and Prince Edward Street. The services were in German, and German was frequently spoken in the neighbourhood.

According to an account by Joe Swan, Helen had complained to a number of her relatives that her current employer was a Communist and that other Communists would gather in the shop where she worked. It was also rumoured that drugs were sold at the store, wrote Swan, but that was never substantiated.

Police believe that the murders occurred late on Tuesday, June 10. When Helen failed to show up to work the next day, her boss tried to call David at his job. When he learned that neither Helen nor David had reported to work, he called police.

Dorothy's friend, twelve-year-old Edel Friesen, was likely the last person to see Dorothy and her father alive. She told a reporter that she had dropped by that day and found her friend practicing the piano. They talked for a little while, and then Edel left around 7:00 p.m. Dorothy, she said, told her she was going to her room to do homework.

Police, Crowds Swarm over Scene of Brutal Triple Murder

Immediately after discovering the bodies, officers cordoned off the house and yard, the adjacent vacant lot on the east side, and a yard and house that was under construction on the west side. Detective Inspector Archie Plummer, Detective Sergeant Bill Morphett, a team of four detectives, six constables, four commando squad members, and police officer Don Hockin and his tracking dog Polar searched through an abandoned car found nearby and through garbage cans and in the brush on the lane for clues and for either the gun or the axe that was used in the murders.

More than 300 people stood outside in shocked silence as ambulance men brought out the three bodies, one at a time. One woman from the area told a reporter that she had chained her doors ever since the murder of Evelyn Roche. She said she would now use tables and chairs to barricade her doors until the killer was captured.

Detective Sergeant Percy Easler, head of the police science bureau, supervised a team of forensics staff as they collected blood samples from the shoe print, David's blood-stained fedora hat, and other evidence from the home. Their house was dusted for fingerprints.

Detectives had found "DP & HT" scribbled in a young person's writing in six-inch (15.24-cm) high letters on the Pauls' back door. It's unlikely the fastidious and strict David Pauls would have left it there very long, and it was never determined whether Dorothy ("DP") or someone else—either the boy himself or school friends—did this as a prank to tease Dorothy about a boy she may have liked.

It's possible that she was having problems, perhaps because of her strict Mennonite upbringing. At the inquest, Helen's boss, Edward Poloway, testified that Helen had occasionally complained about the treatment Dorothy received at the hands of other children at her school. "She was quite concerned at one time, in connection with a knife being held [at Dorothy's back] at school and some girls saying, 'Kill her, kill her,'" said Poloway. On other occasions, Dorothy had told her mother that children had thrown rocks at her and pulled her hair at school. Poloway said that Helen had told him that Dorothy was also upset that her mother would not let her attend dances or wear lipstick and "fancier" dresses like other girls.

Source: Vancouver Sun, June 12, 1958

Left: Crowds watched as bodies were brought out of the house one at a time.
Right: Don Hockin and Polar, his tracking dog, search for the murder weapon.

At the same time as the forensic team was searching the house, another team visited Dorothy's school and questioned her friends. They wanted to know her habits, what boys she knew, and whether any of them were strong enough to wreak the kind of havoc that they found in the otherwise neat house.

Accounts vary as to the identity of "HT." *The Province* reported that it stood for Harry Troews, a son of family friends who lived in the Fraser Valley. In Joe Swan's account, HT was a young boy at Dorothy's school who was unaware of her crush and who had an alibi.

Police were kept busy chasing several other lines of inquiry. Neighbours reported that a large boy aged around sixteen was seen firing a .22—the same calibre as the murder weapon—at cans on the vacant lot next to the Pauls home six weeks before the murders. Another neighbour reported that he had seen a "crazy" man behind the house on the Saturday night before they were murdered. He said the man walked toward them "yelling crazily." He didn't call police.

Slayer of Family of Three Hunted by All City Police

The only clues police had to go on in the Pauls' murder investigation were a partial footprint in the garden, a bloody but unidentifiable palm print on the wall, and a dislodged rock in the garden that indicated the way the killer had fled.

The murder weapons were never found, but forensics determined that the bullets likely came from a Rohm RG-10 revolver. This was another dead end as the guns were widely sold in drug stores throughout the US for $14.95 under the brand name Rosco.

A neighbour told a *Province* reporter that he saw a blue 1950 Ford parked in the back lane near the Pauls' chicken coop on the night of the murder. A thirteen-year-old boy said he saw a blue car circling the block from his living room window. The driver, he said, was alone and had a moustache. These leads went nowhere.

At one point, police believed they had found their murderer when Bellingham Police arrested Henry Thompson, an eighteen-year-old First Nations boy from Mission, BC, a small town about an hour from Vancouver. Thompson was charged with the attempted rape of Bellingham, Washington, resident Sharon Sharp, aged eleven, and the sexual assault and murder of Ethel Tussing, also of Bellingham, who was walking home after dropping off her daughter at a babysitting job. Ethel died from a fractured skull. The attacks happened four days after the Pauls were murdered, and newspapers of the time reported that Thompson had come to Bellingham via Vancouver. That fact that his initials were the same as the ones found scratched on the Pauls' back door seemed a bizarre coincidence. Although the murders were similar, police told reporters that Thompson was on Vancouver Island at the time of the Pauls' murders.

Police followed up on a number of leads, but couldn't find a motive. A botched robbery and a potential home invasion were ruled out because while David's wallet was missing along with his house keys, it contained only a small amount of money. Nothing else in the house was ransacked or even touched, including Helen's purse, which lay open on the table. Police later found several hundred dollars hidden in jars and socks. The robbery made sense if David was killed because he offered resistance, but it couldn't explain why a thief would also kill Dorothy and Helen. Thieves rarely carried guns.

Another theory was that Dorothy was the target all along. A peeping Tom had been reported in the area around the same time, and there was the partial footprint outside her window. Police had investigated a series of reports of peeping Toms in the area and theorized that the peeper was caught by David as he watched Dorothy undress. As with the robbery theory, it seemed unlikely that a peeper would carry a gun and then wait around and take out the entire family. More than likely he would have fled.

Neighbours speculated that it may have been a case of mistaken identity. The Pauls had bought the house from long-time residents Charles Geach, a police sergeant with the Vancouver police department, and his wife Violet. At fifty-three, Geach was the same age as David Pauls and also had a daughter. Geach said that he had never met the Pauls.

Problems from Russia?

The Pauls were devout Mennonites but had broken away from the church after David refused to tithe a percentage of his earnings. Former Vancouver police sergeant Joe Swan noted that some Mennonites told him that the killings were "the will of God" and refused to assist police. Mennonites generally harboured a deep distrust and suspicion of police, but their lack of cooperation with the investigators and the loss of a small tithe were hardly a motive for a triple murder.

Another theory was that the Pauls had left behind an unresolved problem in their native Russia that had followed them to Vancouver. According to Joe Swan's account, Helen's father was murdered during the Russian Revolution. The problem with this theory was that David had lived in Canada for thirty-five years, Helen for twenty-nine—they were teenagers when they arrived in Canada. Swan also published a rambling letter that police had received during the investigation, which sounded like it was written by someone who did not

Courtesy Vancouver Police Museum

Crime scene photo, June 1958.

have English as a first language. The letter was addressed to the Chief of Police and said: "Dear Sir: The man you should go after for the murders is [name blanked out]. He once told me that was [his] house and someday it would be his. He knew what he was doing had everything arranged to look like a robbery etc. he is a cunning crook. Stop looking for innocent schoolboys and question him. He is the one. A one-time friend."

Swan says rather than ignore this bizarre letter, police investigated because the name of the suspect, a Russian man whom the Pauls had stayed with when they first came to Vancouver, had come up at another point in their investigation. Police took palm prints, which didn't match the print left on the wall, and administered a polygraph test, which the suspect passed.

A revenge killing made sense, given the brutality of the murders—but then, why not shoot Dorothy as well? And why beat all three after they were dead, unless the killer was trying to send some kind of a message?

The Pauls family has always believed that David, Helen, and Dorothy were murdered by the Russian mob because Helen overheard something she shouldn't have at work. The shoelace that was tied around David's wrist, they thought, was the signature of Russian criminals.

Police looked into the theory that Helen, David, or even Dorothy could have been the main target. The 1958 police department annual report noted that the "investigation failed to indicate any definite motive. It is believed that one member of the family may have been the target, but it was necessary to kill all three since any of the others could have probably identified the killer."

The murder weapons were never found.

Courtesy Vancouver Police Department

In June 2015, 57 years after the murders, the Vancouver Police Department added the Pauls to its cold cases website, *vpdcoldcases.ca*.

In the end, police interviewed more than 3,000 relatives, associates, and friends from the Pauls' past and present. "Numerous anonymous letters have been received and the leads investigated, and all murder cases since then have been carefully compared but no definite motive has been established and no suspects have been indicated," said the report.

As horrific as the murders were, five days later, a new event took over the front pages of the newspapers, and the Pauls disappeared from sight. On June 17, 1958, the Second Narrows Bridge collapsed, plunging seventy-nine workers into the water below. Eighteen men and a diver who was searching for bodies died.

A packed service was held for the Pauls at the MEI Auditorium in Abbotsford on June 21 at 2:00 p.m. The family was buried at the Hazelwood Cemetery.

A $14,000 reward offered by Woodward's Department Store, the *Vancouver Sun*, the Vancouver Police Commission, radio station CKNW, and Mayor Fred Hume for identifying the murderer was never claimed.

Sources:
Globe and Mail: June 13, 1958
Province: June 12, 14, 16, 1958
Vancouver Sun: June 12, 17, 18, 1958
West Ender: November 24; December 1, 1983

*Eighteen months after the Pauls brutal murders, Lila Anderson's badly
beaten body was found less than a mile (1.3 km) from their house.
Like Helen Pauls and Evelyn Roche, she also was travelling by bus,
and while Evelyn was murdered just hours before Easter Friday,
Lila was murdered on Christmas night.*

CHAPTER 8

The Yuletide Murder

On Boxing Day morning in 1959, Jackie Hunter, aged ten, and Colin Woodward, eight, were out walking their dog on city-owned land at Knight Street and 45th Avenue when they came across the naked body of Lila Anderson.

Lila was lying on her back in a ravine of mud and water, her body hidden from the street by a mound of soft earth. Her right arm was extended out, and the only clothes she had on were silk stockings that hung around her ankles and a black skirt, which the killer had wrapped around her head. Her red coat lay nearby, ripped from her body in the struggle.

The boys raced home and brought Bill Hunter, Jackie's father, back to the site. "It was an awful shock for the boys," Hunter told a reporter. "I'm still shaking myself."

Hunter managed to flag down a police car. When Constable Falconer climbed down the ravine he checked the body for a pulse, and finding none, he immediately called for assistance.

Police found a large rock next to Lila's body covered in blood and human tissue. Another pile of rocks near the body was splattered with blood stains and human tissue, suggesting that the murderer may have smashed her head against them. Police found Lila's purse in a pool of water nearby, its contents—a BC Electric bill, a little over three dollars in change, and a bank-account book—strewn on the ground.

An autopsy the next day determined that Lila died after receiving multiple heavy blows to the head delivered with such force that her skull was severely fractured. All of the cuts showed ragged edges, and with the massive fragmentation of bone, the pathologist determined that a heavy, blunt instrument, possibly a tire iron, had caused the injuries. There was evidence of a sexual attack, but rape couldn't be determined because she was so badly beaten. Time of death was fixed at Christmas night, only an hour or so after she'd eaten steak and onions for dinner.

Nobody Knew Lila Well

Lila was originally from Rock Creek, a small British Columbia Interior town located between Osoyoos and Grand Forks. Her parents were dead, and she had two brothers and a sister living in the Interior. Lila had left home and worked in a Penticton restaurant for a while, but when World War II broke out, she joined the Royal Canadian Air Force as a sergeant cook serving in Eastern Canada.

After she was discharged in 1945, Lila moved to Vancouver and became the assistant night manager at the White Lunch restaurant. About five years before her murder, she took a job as a cashier for the Safeway at Broadway and Main Street.

Newspaper pictures show an attractive and pleasant looking thirty-eight-year-old woman with brown eyes and brown hair streaked with grey. At the inquest she was described as a "well nourished, well developed female" standing just over five feet, five inches tall and weighing 130 pounds (59 kg).

Relatives and friends painted a picture of a quiet woman who liked her own company and preferred to live alone. She laughed at funny things, they said, was friendly to small children, and had a nice smile.

Lila first appears in the city directories in 1947 living on West 8th Avenue. By 1950 she had bought a property at 30 East 15th Avenue. She drew up her own blueprints for a boarding house, hired a construction crew, and supervised the work. When it was finished, she moved into the bottom suite and rented out the upstairs.

Ian McHattie, a contractor who worked on Lila's house, told a reporter: "She knew more about plumbing and carpentry than any woman I know." McHattie said that another man who worked for Lila had asked for a date, but she refused him. He said when he arrived at work on two occasions, she was having coffee with the worker and seemed fond of him.

Lila was friendly to her customers and neighbours and enjoyed talking about her house and garden, but otherwise kept to herself. Her fiancé was killed in Germany during the war, and her family told reporters that she didn't date and showed no interest in men. She made it clear that her private life was her own business, and she expected her neighbours and friends to respect that. What they did know was that Lila loved to garden; she loved Mikie, her eight-year-old black and white cat, and she was happy to stay at home listening to the radio or watching television. As far as anyone knew, she had no close friends.

"Lila was the nicest kind of a girl," her sister Veda told reporters. "She never was one to live it up or to go out on the town. She wasn't the kind to be afraid of the dark or of being alone. She worked six years at the White Lunch on Hastings and left to walk home every night at 1:30 a.m. She was never afraid."

In the Vancouver of 1959, a fiercely independent, single, and capable woman was clearly an enigma to family, friends, and the media.

Murderer Eludes Massive Police Search

The east side of Vancouver was experiencing a wave of violence against women in the late 1950s. The week before Lila's murder, fifteen-year-old Joan Pallot was grabbed and stabbed twice in the back after she got off a bus at 9:00 p.m. in the 1000 block of East 54th Avenue. On the Monday night following Lila's murder, twenty-year-old Mary Bonk was attacked a mile (1.6 km) from where Lila's body was found, and just three blocks from the Pauls house. Mary told police she was on her way home to her house on East 44th Avenue at 10:00 p.m. when she was attacked walking to the bus stop on Main Street. She screamed and ran, she said, and her attacker fled in a late-model car.

This photo of Lila Anderson ran in the newspaper under the heading "Are you a hidden witness?"

At first glance, there didn't seem to be much in common between the murder of Evelyn Roche in April 1958, the Pauls family three months later, and Lila Anderson the following year. But the media made the link, drawing a terror map that showed the proximity of the Pauls' house to where Lila's body was found as well as the knife attack on the school girl. Aside from the brutality and the proximity of the murders, there were other similarities. Evelyn, Lila, and Helen were all coming home after taking a bus at night. None of the victims were robbed. Dorothy and Lila both had their heads wrapped after they were killed, and Dorothy, Lila, and Evelyn were either partially or completely stripped, yet there was no evidence of rape.

There was another possible connection. Before the Pauls bought their house on East 53rd Avenue, they stayed with a Mennonite family on East 44th Avenue. City directories show that a couple called the Boughs lived two doors down. In 1958 Arthur Bough, a porter with the Canadian Pacific Railway, and his wife Mildred were shown to be living at Lila's boarding house. At the time of her death, they were her only tenants.

Surely Someone Saw Her

Lila had attended the midnight service at Christ Church Cathedral on Christmas Eve. Police appealed through the media to anyone who might have seen Lila wearing a beige-coloured hat with gold trim, sitting with somebody at the service.

The major problem for police was trying to establish a timeline for Lila's murder and to find out with whom she'd had dinner on Christmas Eve. The media ran her photo in the newspapers and a description of her clothes—her favourite red coat with leopard-skin lining. Friends told police that she walked like a queen with a regal bearing, but even with this description and media photographs of the clothes she was wearing at the time of her death, police were unable to find anyone who saw her after she left home on Christmas Day. Lila had told several neighbours and family members that she had plans for Christmas dinner, but was vague about the details. She talked to her sister Veda at 2:00 p.m. on Christmas Day. "I phoned her at her boarding house, and she told me then she was just going out to have Christmas dinner. I was going to ask her where and with whom, but she didn't say and I didn't ask," Veda told a reporter. She said the impression Lila gave her was that she was going out for dinner with several friends. "I think the friends had been working like herself and didn't have time to get dinner so they all went to a restaurant," she said. "Lila would have ordered a steak like she usually did."

Veda's son Bud studied hairdressing and was staying with Lila while he went to school. He told his mother that Lila had bought a twenty-pound (nine-kg) turkey on sale the week before, and that they were both sick of turkey.

Lila's next door neighbour Anita Quenneville phoned her around 3:00 p.m. to thank her for a Christmas gift and to ask her over to visit the next day. "She sounded happy," said the neighbour. "She said she would come, but she was in a hurry just then because she was going out for dinner with friends."

Lila's tenant, Mildred Bough, told police that she heard Lila moving about downstairs around 5:00 p.m. on Christmas afternoon. All the neighbours were canvassed, but no one saw her leave home that evening.

Lilly Padgham was a friend of Lila's who had served with her in the RCAF. She told a reporter that she highly doubted that Lila was out on a date. If she was, said Lilly, Lila would have insisted on being picked up at her house. "She was probably forcibly picked up while she was waiting for the bus in the area where she was killed," Lilly told a reporter, adding that she thought it would take more than one person to kill Lila. "She was so strong, and she could fight back. Knowing Lila, she would, too. She didn't have much use for men." Added her brother Albert: "She was very strong. Whoever did it would have to get the first crack in."

Detectives also considered that she made up the story about dining with friends so she could spend Christmas alone. And because she ate steak and not more traditional Christmas fare, police believe she had eaten out at a restaurant shortly before she was killed.

Police Deplore Lack of Witnesses

A bus driver came forward and said he thought he had seen her on his bus, travelling from Broadway and Main Street to 41st Avenue and Main at about 5:00 p.m. on Christmas Day.

When police went knocking on doors around 45th Avenue and Knight Street, a few residents told them they had heard screams a little after 6:00 p.m., but no one had thought to call police.

From the evidence that they could gather, police believe the first attack on Lila started at an unlighted bus stop where they found a patch of blood and hair on the ground. She was then likely forced into a car and driven a short distance down 45th Avenue and onto the field, which locals said was a popular lover's lane. Investigators analyzed the impression of a set of tire marks which entered the site from 45th Avenue and appeared to go where the glove and buttons were found, then turn around and go back the same way.

The second attack, they say, came after she had been taken to the vacant lot by car. She was dragged from the car and in the struggle lost her coat, glove, and white buttons from her blouse. Further into the field were the marks of the third attack, where her bra and underwear were ripped from her body. Police also found samples of hair and blood and scrapings from Lila's fingernails at the murder scene.

Police said it had all the earmarks of a sex killing. "It is a dreadful commentary on a type of city as ours that such a crime could occur," Chief George Archer told the media. "Someone must have seen her travelling about the city, or at her Christmas dinner. Yet not one single witness has come forward to help the investigation."

Sources:
Globe and Mail: December 27, 1959
Province: December 28, 30, 1959
Vancouver Sun: December 28, 29, 1959
West Ender: January 1, 1987; May 14, 1992

In 1967 Nancy Johnsen, seven, was plucked from her front yard
in Cloverdale, strangled, and her body dumped in a ravine near her house.
Two years later, Evangeline Azarcon, also seven, disappeared on
the way home from her west side school. In 1972 Tanya Busch, another
seven-year-old, was abducted from the grounds of her east side school.
The bodies of all three little girls were found in Surrey. While Tanya's killer
was convicted, Nancy and Evangeline's murders remained unsolved.

CHAPTER 9

The Cloverdale Abduction

Cloverdale, part of Surrey, BC, is only about twenty-five miles (forty kilometres) from Vancouver, yet it still has a small-town feel and enough farmland to give it a rural flavour. It's known for the annual rodeo held there each May.

In the 1960s, the Johnsen family grew cucumbers and raised chickens and a couple of cows on their five-acre (two-hectare) property on 78 Avenue in Cloverdale. Forty-one-year-old Irvan Johnsen was a carpenter at the Surrey School Board and had gradually added on to his rambling farmhouse as his family grew. In 1967 he and Shirley had seven sons and three daughters ranging in age from baby Tom to sixteen-year-old William.

Courtesy Margaret and Mary Johnsen

Nancy Johnsen, aged seven, at the farm in Cloverdale in 1967.

Daughter Nancy was a happy seven-year-old girl with short dark hair. She loved to play with her dolls, play tag or hide-and-seek with her brothers and sisters, and be outdoors.

On Tuesday, November 7, 1967, the boisterous Johnsen family had finished dinner and several of the kids were playing around the house. It was a big deal for the younger ones to get the newspaper from the mailbox at the end of the driveway each night, and this night it was Nancy's turn. Nancy told her mother she was going out to get the newspaper.

"I remember it was after supper, and we were all going to play hide-and-seek in the house," recalls Mary, Nancy's older sister. "We were playing and we were wondering why Nancy wasn't playing with us, and then we started to look for her."

Missing

When the Johnsens couldn't find her, they checked the backyard and then the front of the house. Then they phoned their neighbours.

It was a dark November night, and one by one the neighbours told them that they hadn't seen Nancy that day. At 6:45 p.m. Irvan Johnsen phoned the RCMP, who quickly mobilized searchers. Within hours tracker dogs and more than 100 nearby residents and volunteers formed a search party and scoured the countryside around the Johnsen property.

"Whoever did it must have led her past the house to the rear of the property," Irvan Johnsen told a reporter. "It was odd we never heard anything. One of my boys had tied up our dog about 4:30 p.m., but we never heard the dog bark. I guess it didn't hear anything either."

Harry De Boer, the Johnsen's thirteen-year-old neighbour, said he delivered the Johnsen's paper at 5:10 p.m. He told police he didn't see anything unusual. Today, the once-rural area where the Johnsens lived has grown into a bedroom community for Vancouver. Large modern houses line 78 Avenue where the Johnsen's had their cucumber farm, and what was then a dirt road. Behind the hilly property were fields and a peat bog, once used for duck hunting. Now, most of that land belongs to the Surrey Golf Course, which opened in 1971.

Police called off the search at 2:30 a.m., but the Johnsens couldn't sleep and searched throughout the night. The full-scale search resumed at dawn, when police arrived with dogs.

Nancy's grandfather found her shoes with the laces tied together hanging from a fence near the house. At 7:45 a.m. searchers found her little body lying face down in a marshy area by a creek less than a quarter of a mile (0.3 km) from the Johnsen home.

RCMP officers and ambulance attendants carry body of Nancy Johnsen from ravine where it was found.

Tragedy lay beyond door

Province, November 8, 1967

RCMP officers and ambulance attendants carry the body of Nancy Johnsen from the ravine where she was found.

The white blouse and blue skirt she was wearing were in disarray, and her panties were missing, but she had not been sexually assaulted. An RCMP officer told reporters that marks indicated that she had been dragged along the ground. Her stomach was full, indicating that her death occurred within two hours after she had eaten dinner. The cause of death was strangulation; her body also showed multiple lacerations and abrasions.

Mary, who was nine, remembers the black cars that came for her sister's body. "Because I was the oldest daughter, my mum said for me to keep the little ones away from the window. So I kept the little ones away from the window, but I looked," she says.

Police Hunt Child Killer

The file of newspaper clippings about Nancy Johnsen's murder is thin, but even so the frustration of the RCMP officers is palpable. RCMP inspector W.R. Morrison told reporters that the investigation had been hampered because the murderer's tracks were obliterated by the dozens of police and searchers who combed the marshy area looking for the little girl.

Morrison, who headed up a fourteen-man team investigating the murder, questioned neighbours in an effort to find out her last movements. "We haven't come up with anything so far," he said. "We have absolutely no leads at the moment."

"She was the prettiest little girl you'd want to meet, always obliging and eager to please," her teacher Eleanor Johnson told a reporter. "She was the happiest child I've seen." Nancy was one of thirty-four students in Miss Johnson's class at the William Watson elementary school.

Margaret was only six when her sister Nancy was murdered. "It was very horrific, very damaging for all of us. It caused a ripple throughout all our lives," she says. "We were just never safe again." Margaret, Nancy, and their older sister Mary were very close—only three years apart in age from youngest to oldest. "Everybody called us 'the three girls,'" says Margaret. "And it was so weird after Nancy passed away. I became part of the 'four little ones.'"

Everything changed for the Johnsens after the murder. "Nancy's murder affected my mum and dad so horrifically. My mum was in a depression for the rest of her life," says Margaret. "But she was a good mother to us. She still managed to keep the house and cook our meals and take care of us, and I give her so much credit for that. I don't know if I could go on, not knowing who hurt my child." Shirley, who was thirty-eight when Nancy was murdered, gave birth to a little boy eighteen months later. The baby lived for only four days. It was a terrible blow for Shirley, a devout Catholic. She asked her priest to grant her absolution so that she could stop having children. He said no. "So we left the church, but I remember how difficult that was for my mum, not to attend church anymore," says Margaret.

Focus on Family

The police didn't help. They focussed their investigation on the family, accusing the older brothers and even Shirley herself. "It was almost abusive," says Margaret. "The police never led us to believe that they looked outside the family."

Neil Boyd, director of the School of Criminology at Simon Fraser University, says it's not surprising that police investigations always start with the family. "Up to ninety percent of murders take place between people who know each other very well," he says.

Historically, victims are murdered by family members for money or in the heat of passion, by jealous lovers, or by friends or work colleagues for some grievance that's either real or imagined. The motive is usually easily detected, and the killer often leaves a trail of evidence behind. "The reality is that most often a child is killed by a family member, most often the father, second, the mother, and third the siblings. That's more common than a predatory attack by a stranger, so it's understandable that police thought that was more logical," says Boyd.

Boyd says that, on average, ten percent of murders are unsolved in any given year. "When we get into unsolved homicides, a lot higher percentage of those involve the killing of strangers, and when we think about the killing of strangers, serial killings that are sexually motivated are the single most significant category." After Nancy's death, the Johnsen farm became a kind of morbid tourist attraction. The Johnsens were horrified when strangers would appear on their property and even park in their driveway. "My dad called them prowlers," says Margaret. "It was just so weird that these people thought it was okay to come." After a few years, Irvan built a house in the rural community of Aldergrove, BC, and moved his family there.

Mary Johnsen says that one of the hardest things to deal with was that Nancy's murder was never spoken about when they were growing up. "My parents never, ever talked about it," she says. "My mum had a wreath from my sister's funeral in her bedroom. We saw it every time we went into the bedroom, but we didn't talk about it. We were never allowed to discuss it."

More tragedy followed several years later when Margaret's friend and neighbour, fifteen-year-old Theresa Hildebrandt, went missing in 1976. Police treated the case as a runaway, and it wasn't until her remains were found in a shallow grave in a gully four years later that police realized they were dealing with a murder case. Theresa's murder was linked to two others—that of eleven-year-old Kathryn-Mary Herbert, who went missing in September 1975 from Abbotsford, and Monica Jack, aged twelve, who disappeared while riding her bike near Merritt, BC, in 1978. Monica's remains wouldn't be found for another seventeen years.

Police had long had Gary Taylor Handlen on their radar, but it took them more than three decades to get the evidence to charge the convicted rapist with the murders of Kathryn-Mary and Monica. At the time of writing, police didn't have enough evidence to charge Handlen with Theresa's murder, and her case remains unsolved.

Irvan Johnsen retired after thirty years with the Surrey School Board, and he and Shirley moved to Lamont, Alberta, to be closer to Margaret's growing young family. But tragedy struck the Johnsen family yet again in June of 1998 when Irvan and Shirley were killed in a car accident when a driver made an illegal left-hand turn in front of them. The couple were on their way to the Banff National Park to celebrate their forty-eighth wedding anniversary.

Three of Margaret's older brothers have also passed away; one committed suicide.

The police never closed Nancy's case. Every year, for almost half a century, they would re-question the family until Margaret finally asked them to stop. "They were calling me up until a year ago and asking me if there was anything new that I remembered, and I finally asked them to just stop calling me," she says. "There's nothing more to say to them. I think they got it wrong right from the beginning."

Sources:
Edmonton Journal: June 6, 1998
Surrey Leader: November 9, 1967
Vancouver Sun: November 7, 1967

"Predatory, serial sexual attacks are very rare, and when there's a similarity and character over a relatively short period of time, that tends to point to the likelihood that we are looking for the same person," says Neil Boyd, director of the School of Criminology at Simon Fraser University.

CHAPTER 10

Second Seven-Year-Old Goes Missing

On Thursday, November 20, 1969, two years after the murder of Nancy Johnsen in Cloverdale, Evangeline Azarcon disappeared on the way home from school in Vancouver. Her abduction sparked the biggest search in BC's history.

The Azarcons had moved to Vancouver from Manila in the Philippines, a little over three years before. Alejandro, a thirty-five-year-old mechanical engineer, worked for Canadian Comstock. "We came to Canada for the sake of the children," a distraught Alejandro told a reporter after his daughter went missing. "My Canadian boss in Manila told us about the good chances here, and it is true. There are so many schools, playgrounds, parks."

It was, however, a move he began to regret as he paced the worn rug in his living room, waiting for word about Evangeline, a grade-two student at Edith Cavell Elementary.

Province, June 26, 1978

Evangeline
Azarcon, 1969.

Eve Lazarus photo, 2015

Edith Cavell Elementary school where Evangeline attended grade two in 1969.

Evangeline was the second eldest of five children. Her brothers, nine-year-old Armando and five-year-old Eric, and sisters Mercy, aged four, and Cynthia, two, lived with their father and mother, Corazon, in a duplex at the corner of West 19th Avenue and Laurel Street.

Just the day before her disappearance, Corazon Azarcon had made Evangeline stay home from school because the little girl had a cold. When Evangeline became upset at being kept away from school for another day, her mother relented and let her go.

Evangeline, a petite and pretty seven-year-old with short black hair and dark eyes, walked the four blocks to school with her friend and next-door neighbour Caroline Cruz. She dressed that morning in a red sweater and matching red shoes, the faded brown corduroy jumper her mother had made for her, and a yellow plastic headband topped off with a brown hat with a leather bow. Because it was cold, she wore her winter jacket, a green checkered coat with an imitation black fur collar. Her mother packed her red plaid lunch box with chocolate milk, potato chips, a pear, a boiled egg, and a sandwich.

While normally the girls would walk home together, on that particular afternoon, Caroline was kept late at school and Evangeline went home alone.

Eve Lazarus photo, 2015

Evangeline was last seen walking past this park at Heather and 19th Avenue at 3:15 p.m. on her way home from school.

She was last seen at about 3:15 p.m. near Heather Street and 19th Avenue—about half-way between the school and her house.

If Evangeline was going to a friend's place to play after school, she always asked her mother first. And while sometimes she would stop to collect leaves and sticks, she was always home well before dark—and never home later than 4:00 p.m. Since the family had splurged on a colour television a few months before, Evangeline had arrived home promptly at 3:15 p.m. every day to watch her favourite cartoon show. So when Evangeline hadn't arrived home by 4:00 p.m., Corazon started to worry. She called Evangeline's friends, but no one had seen the little girl.

Alejandro came home from work and started to search the neighbourhood. He spent hours looking in the rain, going back and forth between their duplex and the school and walking the blocks around the area. At first he thought she might have either fallen, been hit by a car, or taken a detour and become lost. At 9:00 p.m. he called police.

Search Joined by Thousands

Police did a house-to-house neighbourhood search. Several dog teams were brought in to scour Queen Elizabeth Park as well as the general area where Evangeline was last seen.

"She would not run away from home," Alejandro told a reporter. "She is different from most Canadian children—not so independent. Family ties are very very strong among Filipino families." Later that night, he told a reporter that he hoped to get a call from a kidnapper, just to know that she was all right. Evangeline was a shy little girl who loved to read and play with her brothers and sisters. Her parents said they had told Evangeline not to take candy from strangers but had no idea what she would do if someone offered. "I guess it would depend on the way she was approached," Alejandro told a reporter.

Police asked residents in the area to check their yards, garages, basements, and even garbage cans—anywhere that might offer a potential clue to the little girl's disappearance. The search went on all night, the next day, and continued through the weekend. On the third day of Evangeline's disappearance, police were calling it a possible abduction, and 2,000 people had mobilized to search the city. Volunteers began a phone campaign that attempted to reach every person listed in the 798 pages of the Greater Vancouver telephone directory. By the Tuesday, more than 5,000 people had joined in and were tramping through dense bush in areas as far east as Chilliwack, BC, and as far south as the Blaine–Douglas US border crossing.

As the days passed the search gained momentum. Members of the police and fire departments joined the search on their days off, army units from the

The Azarcons' duplex on West 19th Avenue.

RCAF station at Jericho Beach combed Stanley Park, soldiers from the Chilliwack army base searched the Fraser Valley, local First Nations bands joined in, canoe club members scoured False Creek, Richmond gun club members searched Lulu, Sea, and Iona Islands while members of other boating clubs searched waterways, and members of the North Vancouver Ski Patrol searched the Mount Seymour region.

University professors cancelled classes, and more than 3,500 students from the University of BC and Simon Fraser University hunted through the bush that surrounded those institutions. High school students from Vancouver College, Notre Dame, and St. Thomas Aquinas soon joined in the search, while North Shore students were released from classes to help police check out leads in their area.

More than 300 ham radio operators, scouts, cubs, cadets, and ambulance crews offered assistance. Okanagan Helicopters donated a helicopter, BC Telephone installed special lines into search headquarters near the Azarcon home, and a local supermarket supplied coffee and cookies to volunteers.

A Dutch clairvoyant named Gerard Croiset was even called in to help find Evangeline. "We know it sounds like a slim chance, but he's found people all over the place," a searcher told a reporter. "We're desperate right about now."

Rewards for information leading to her return totalled $5,000, including $1,000 from her father's employer, Canadian Comstock. By the time the official search was called off on December 12, close to 50,000 people had searched bush, back streets, mountains, beaches, and river banks. More than eighty organizations had participated. Evangeline had literally disappeared without a trace. And it would take another two months before the Azarcon family would get an answer.

Mounted Vancouver police constables Gary Larsen, left, on Gunner, and Harold Newcomb on Soldier, search brush in Stanley Park for Evangeline Azarcon.

Province, November 25, 1969

Missing Girl Found Dead

At 9:30 a.m. on January 20, 1970, a farmer in Port Kells, a neighbourhood in the city of Surrey, BC, was walking through an abandoned mill site that adjoined his property when he found a child's red lunch box with Evangeline's name inside it. He called police.

Police scoured the property, a marshy area dotted with pools and drainage ditches and screened by scrubby trees that was frequently flooded by the nearby Fraser River. Two hours into the search, a police officer found a child's red shoe at the edge of a pond surrounded by swamp and willows. Minutes later, RCMP Constable Alfred Erickson found a small body lying face down in a drainage trench flooded by about two feet (sixty cm) of water. Evangeline was still dressed in the clothes she wore the day she went missing. It was two months to the day after she'd disappeared.

The area, which had once been a sawdust dump on the mill property, bordered the Canadian National Railway at 192nd Street and Margaret Road, about a third of a mile (half a km) south of the Trans-Canada Highway. Police believe that she had been left on dry ground and her body had been covered with old firewood and scrap. Later, the area had flooded, leaving her in a pool of water from the nearby river.

After Evangeline's body was taken away, police sealed off the area and searched the frozen pond with rakes and hooks attached to long iron rods to crack the ice and look for evidence. A grader and three ditch diggers arrived from the City of Surrey to lower the level of the pond in the hope of finding more clues to the identity of the killer.

An autopsy showed that Evangeline had died the day she was abducted—between four and ten hours after eating the lunch her mother had packed for her. She had been sexually assaulted, there was bruising around her head and a cut above her left eye, and she had either drowned or had choked to death on her stomach contents.

Evangeline's body was placed in a little white coffin and returned to the Philipines to be buried in Manila.

After Evangeline's body was found, the case moved into the hands of the Surrey RCMP's Criminal Investigation Branch. For the first two weeks of the investigation, the entire Surrey plainclothes detail of eighteen men worked night and day, assisted by several uniformed officers. After the first month, the detail was reduced to eight plus Staff Sergeant Bud Domay, who headed the investigation. By August, the investigation comprised three plainclothes men and a fourth officer undertaking a reinvestigation.

Herb Pittman, a garage owner near the site where Evangeline was found, told police he had seen three cars parked in the area around the time she had disappeared. Thirteen-year-old Brian Bussiere, who lived across the road from the site, told a *Province* reporter that he had seen a man driving a red and white 1959 Chevrolet in the area five times in recent weeks, the last time about ten days before Evangeline's body was discovered in January 1970. "He would go to a different place and stay up to three hours every time he came," Bussiere said. "He just sat and looked. It was weird. There's not much interesting to look at there—just what used to be a gravel pit in an old dump or something."

The twenty-acre site was still used as a dump by locals. In recent years, it had also become a popular "lover's lane" and this caused problems for police because, as one resident noted, "Cars going down there could be perfectly innocent so far as the murder is concerned."

Police Step Up Hunt for Sexual Predator
Police concentrated the search on sexual predators with connections to the area where the Azarcon's lived and to the site where Evangeline's body was found.

One theory that the police developed was that the murderer worked in Vancouver but lived in Surrey and was familiar with the dump site. The logic was that there were plenty of isolated spots between Vancouver and Surrey where she could have been attacked and dumped, but he picked the isolated spot near the Fraser River for a reason.

Neil Boyd, director of the School of Criminology at Simon Fraser University, says that people generally like to operate within their comfort zone, and that's particularly true of criminals. "Criminals tend to commit their crimes in areas that they know well, and so you can look at where a sequence of crimes occur, and you can begin to get a sense from that geography of where the offender is likely to live," he says. "Geographic profiling allows you to narrow the spatial map and look for somebody in that area who may have a previous criminal record relating to sex crimes."

Police checked known pedophiles who targeted girls aged six to eleven and were out on parole. They checked Riverview mental hospital and the prisons for men who were out on a pass on November 20, and they checked their movements. They checked every lead, every hint, every phone call until the individual mentioned was cleared, and they added the results to the Azarcon murder file.

In November of 1970, police said they were looking for "a Caucasian of medium- to small-build and of medium to blond colouring." Sergeant Domay told reporters that the conclusions were the result of "scientific eliminations."

In January 1971, a year after the body was found, police said they had two prime suspects. But both were eliminated.

No connection was made to Nancy Johnsen's murder two years before, at least not in the media. But in 1972, police figured they had their man following the killing of Tanya Busch, whose body was also found in Surrey. Bizarrely, police could not find out if Tanya's killer was out of jail when Evangeline was abducted. "Prison authorities simply couldn't tell us," Murray Scott, the new investigator on the case told *Province* reporter Don Hunter in June 1978. "They don't know."

More than eight years after Evangeline's murder, police had questioned thousands of men in Canada, the United States, and other parts of the world. "On each of the men there is a report, usually terse and single spaced, and most end with 'terminated; no further investigation,'" wrote Hunter in June

1978. "The reports occupy a three-foot [0.91-m] thickness of folders in the General Investigation Section of the Surrey RCMP detachment in Cloverdale ... It's the thickest file they've got in Surrey and under 'present status' it reads 'not cleared.'"

"It'll never be closed," investigator Scott told Hunter, "Never."

Province, June 26, 1978

The police file is still open on the murder of Evangeline Azarcon.

Sources:
Province: November 22, 25, 1969; January 21, 29; November 21, 1970; June 26, 1978
Surrey Leader: January 22, 24, 1970
Vancouver Echo: December 31, 1996
Vancouver Sun: November 22, 24, 26, 1969; January 21, 23, 1970

The murder of seven-year-old Tanya Busch was solved shortly after it was committed. While it may seem strange to include her story in a book about unsolved murders, I believe that there is strong circumstantial evidence to suggest that the same man murdered Tanya Busch, Nancy Johnsen, and Evangeline Azarcon.

CHAPTER 11

The Prison Guard's Daughter

The third seven-year-old girl to be abducted, murdered, and dumped in Surrey in less than five years was Tanya Busch, the daughter of Klaus Busch, a prison guard. Where Nancy Johnsen was taken from her front porch and Evangeline Azarcon was abducted while walking home from school, Tanya, a shy, quiet little girl who loved to read, was taken from outside her school just before classes started one Friday morning in June 1972, less than two miles (3.1 km) from Edith Cavell Elementary, which Evangeline Azarcon had also attended. Unlike the two other little girls who appeared to have vanished into thin air, several witnesses saw Tanya being put into a car, and they were able to describe her abductor.

Thirty-three-year-old Klaus Busch and his wife Ingrid, aged twenty-nine, had moved to Vancouver from Germany six years before. They lived with their two children, Tanya and her little brother Ralph, in a duplex at the corner of Clark Drive and East Fourteenth Avenue in Vancouver, seven blocks from Charles Dickens Elementary School.

Eve Lazarus photo, 2015

The Buschs lived at this Clark Drive duplex in 1972.

Tanya was reported missing at 9:10 a.m. after students in her grade-two class said they had seen her playing in Sunnyside Park, across from the school. She didn't answer during roll call.

Klaus Busch combed the area in his car, and his wife searched on foot. School teachers joined in the search, and police were phoned at 10:00 a.m. Busch said that, because of his job as a prison guard at the BC Penitentiary, Tanya knew that she had to tell her parents where she was at all times. "I have had threats," he told a reporter after his daughter went missing. "There isn't an officer there that hasn't. But I can't think of anyone out of jail now that I've had trouble with before."

On the early summer morning when Tanya went missing, the blonde-haired, blue-eyed little girl dressed for school in a red, white, and blue plaid dress, red socks, and sandals. She carried a white knit sweater with a Munich Olympics logo on it as well as a red plastic lunch bucket, and a school library book called *The Happy Lion and the Bear.*

She walked to school with a friend as she normally did. When they arrived, the friends separated, and Tanya was seen playing in a park across from the school. Her friends later told police that they saw Tanya jump off the swing, that she seemed to be crying, and that she started to run in the direction of her house. Police believe that she had realized that she had left her library book somewhere on the way to school and had run back to find it.

Girl Feared Abducted

One of the young witnesses told police that when Tanya was about a block away from the school, she was approached by a man who talked to her, then took her arm and guided her across the road to where his small dark car was parked.

They got in the car and drove away.

Police believe that the man had sympathized with the little girl's plight and offered to help her find the book. Two girls, aged nine and eleven, who knew Tanya, described a man about six feet tall with reddish bushy hair and "very starey" eyes, about twenty-five-

Tanya was playing on the swings at Sunnyside Park across from her elementary school shortly before she was abducted.

Eve Lazarus photo, 2015

years of age. They also told reporters that a man who fit the description had been seen hanging around the school talking to kids in recent weeks.

Deputy Chief Constable Tom Stokes told reporters that the first thing they did after Tanya went missing was to check the field in Surrey where Evangeline Azarcon's body had been found two years before. Police used a helicopter to search the beaches, gulleys, and the hard-to-access areas of Metro Vancouver. Newspapers and radio stations reported Tanya's disappearance, and with the memory of Evangeline's abduction and murder still fresh in their minds, several hundred volunteers joined in a search that covered almost forty percent of Vancouver in house-to-house inquiries over that first weekend.

On June 14, twelve days after she was abducted from outside her school, Tanya's body was found in the heavily wooded area at 168 Street and 108 Avenue in Surrey, about six miles (ten km) from where Evangeline's body had been recovered in 1970, and about five miles (eight km) from where Nancy Johnsen was murdered and dumped. The sites where both Tanya and Evangeline were found could be accessed via the same exit off the Trans-Canada Highway.

Because of the advanced state of decomposition of Tanya's body, her cause of death was never determined, and she was ultimately identified through dental records.

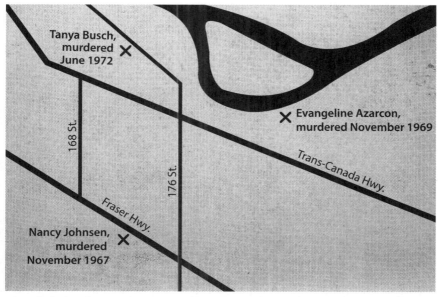

Where the bodies of Nancy Johnsen, Evangeline Azarcon, and Tanya Busch were found in Surrey, BC.

Convicted Rapist Queried

Police suspected that twenty-six-year-old prisoner Charles David Garry Head, who had a toxic relationship with Klaus Busch, murdered Tanya as a revenge killing.

Tanya's body had been found less than half a mile (a third of a km) from Head's mother Annette's house, where he was staying at the time of the murder while on a three-day pass from prison. Police questioned Head several times in prison, dug up the grounds of his mother's house, and searched the well. After Tanya's body was discovered, Head was charged with her murder. He had already been declared a dangerous offender and was supposedly serving life in prison after he was convicted in the rape of two girls aged six and nine in 1967. After the conviction, he was found to be criminally insane and sent to Riverview until his full or partial recovery. Yet just five years later, he was out on a three-day unsupervised "rehabilitation" pass from Agassiz Mountain Prison—his third for the year.

On the day of Tanya's abduction, Head drove his mother in her car to the Guildford Town Centre mall in Surrey where she caught a ride to work. He was last seen driving over the Port Mann Bridge toward Vancouver. Less than an hour after Tanya disappeared, a woman who lived across the street from Annette Head's house said she heard a child crying near their house.

Forensics detectives found cat hairs in the bedroom of the Head house, in the trunk of the car, and on Tanya's clothing, but the Buschs did not own a cat. There was also sawdust in the trunk of the Head car, similar to the sawdust found on the road near the spot where Tanya's body had been found.

Head had asked friends to lie and provide an alibi for the time that Tanya was abducted. He told his mother that he couldn't tell her where he had been because he went to see a drug dealer who wanted him to help rob a bank, and he was afraid that if the authorities found out, he would be sent back to jail. When police went to check up on his alibi, the drug dealer/bank robber denied knowing Head.

Was Convicted Rapist Also a Serial Killer?

Head had been found guilty of rape in May 1967 and declared a dangerous offender six months later, the same month that Nancy Johnsen was raped and murdered. He should have been either in prison or in the Riverview mental hospital two years later when Evangeline Azarcon was murdered, but the prison records were such a mess that police and prosecutors could never determine whether he really was locked up on those dates. "You've got to read in between the lines; there were incomplete records," says former RCMP Staff Sergeant

Fred Bodnaruk. "We found that some of the guards were bribed and that they lied."

(Before Bodnaruk retired in 1976, he headed up the original Unsolved Homicide Unit. He was the principal investigator in the murder case of sixteen-year-old Colleen MacMillan, who had died on the Highway of Tears in 1974 [a section of Highway 16 in north-central British Columbia where a series of unsolved murders and disappearances of young women occurred]. This case was solved nearly forty years after MacMillan's death through DNA testing that linked at least three of the highway murders to Bobby Jack Fowler, an American serial killer who died in an Oregon jail in 2006.)

While Bodnaruk didn't work directly on the murders of the three little girls, he remembers the cases. He believes Head was guilty and that he committed all three murders. "If I'm instrumental in a particular crime, I'll repeat the same system," he explained, "[whether it's] the way you rob a bank or the way you attack a woman. Some rapists will rip your clothes off to rape you, others will hold a knife to your throat so you strip yourself, others will strip your underclothes off or [give you] a severe beating; they get gratification from that. There's always an MO [*modus operandi*]."

Lorraine Shore was a general assignment reporter at the *Vancouver Sun* and later became a lawyer. She covered both Evangeline Azarcon's disappearance and the murder trial of Charles David Garry Head. "I remember the Tanya Busch case quite well," she says. "The prison record-keeping was so bad that they were never sure whether [Head] was actually in or out of prison on particular days."

Head Sentenced to Another Life Term

Head was convicted solely on circumstantial evidence. As a convicted rapist and pedophile already supposedly in prison for life, his guilt would have surprised no one. On the other hand, there were a few holes in the prosecution's case.

As Lorraine Shore points out, three of the witnesses who testified against Head were inmates. Each one testified that Head had told them that he had murdered Tanya Busch because of his hatred of Klaus Busch. Later they recanted. One said his evidence was a "complete fabrication." Another told a newspaper editor that he had made up the testimony against Head because he hated child molesters and was worried that the evidence wasn't strong enough to convict him. "One guy was on the stand three times because he kept changing his story," says Shore. "I imagine that, in the end, nobody believed anything they said. It was quite a case." Shore says that while the evidence against Head was circumstantial, she felt that prosecutor Lee Skipp did a thorough job of tying it all together for the jury.

But as defense counsel Raymond Paris argued unsuccessfully, there were also concerns. The two young girls who witnessed Tanya's abduction said that the man they saw looked like a man who was seen hanging around the school talking to kids. Head wore glasses; the man who abducted Tanya, according to the children's description, did not. Head was also not identified in a line-up. These concerns weren't enough to raise doubt in Head's conviction, and it's possible that he had an accomplice—and there's no doubt that he never should have been let out of jail.

In the end, he was found guilty by a jury of twelve men.

Klaus Busch had no doubts. "I think Head very coldly and calculatedly murdered my daughter," Busch told reporters after the sentencing, adding that he believed the conviction had saved the life of his six-year-old son.

On June 28, 1972, Solicitor-General Jean-Pierre Goyer went on television to announce the indefinite suspension of the temporary leave program for prisoners convicted of sexual offences that he had previously so rigorously defended. "Generally speaking, this program has been highly successful," he told the media. "We goof sometimes."

Charles Head, a child rapist—a man supposedly serving a life sentence—was allowed out on unsupervised passes less than five years after being declared a dangerous offender. And the penal system was so lax and corrupt at that time that there is no way to determine if Head was in or out of jail when Nancy Johnsen and Evangeline Azarcon were murdered.

Now it's unlikely that we will ever know. Charles David Garry Head died of natural causes at the Regional Psychiatric Centre in Saskatoon, Saskatchewan on March 7, 2013. He was sixty-six.

Sources:
Globe and Mail: June 28, 1972; January 23, 25, 27, 1973
Province: June 5, 7, 15, 1972
Vancouver Sun: June 3, 6, 15, 1972; January 24, 1973

"Opportunity is important; so is availability and proximity,"
says Dr Nicole Aube, a Vancouver-based forensic psychologist
who consults with the police about serial killers and sexual offenders.
"We know that people commit more crime in the location where they live."

CHAPTER 12

The Renfrew Murders

Theresa Louise Wise, known as Louise to her friends, turned seventeen the week before she was murdered. A grade-eleven student at Windermere Secondary School, Louise was the eldest of four children and lived in a working-class area of East Vancouver, on Lillooet Street near 16th Avenue. Her father, Jack Wise, was a constable with the Vancouver Police Department.

A photo that ran in the newspapers at the time of her death shows a serious-looking girl with brown hair pulled back off a face hidden behind large, round dark-framed glasses. Louise's friends knew her as a friendly, hard-working, and deeply religious girl who was a member of the Future Nurses Club, participated in Bible study class, and volunteered at the hospital. Unlike most teenage girls, Louise never wore makeup, dressed quite plainly, and never, to anyone's knowledge, had a boyfriend.

In the summer of 1971, Louise was hired as a flower girl for H & T Florists and became one of the ubiquitous teens stationed with flower carts outside liquor stores and hospitals throughout the city. Louise had convinced her parents to let her stay at home by herself while they took the younger children on a family vacation to Birch Bay, just south of White Rock, BC, in Washington state.

The Wises left for their holiday on Saturday, July 7, and Louise worked a 1:00 p.m. to 8:00 p.m. shift outside St. Paul's Hospital.

Last Seen at Sunday Night Church Service

Except for the people Louise saw at a church service near her home on Sunday night, the last known person to see her alive was Gail Hardaker. Gail lived a few doors down from Louise and had known her for most of her life. Even though they went to different elementary schools—Louise attended St. Jude's, the Catholic school—they were always in and out of each other's houses, playing ping pong in the Wises' rec room, or playing with Barbies at Gail's. In the summer, there was always something to do at nearby Renfrew Park where there was a playground, a small outdoor swimming pool, and group activities that ranged from decorating bikes to painting.

Louise Wise (third from left) at Gail Hardaker's birthday party in 1960.

Louise Wise (front with lollipop) at Gail Hardaker's birthday in 1965.

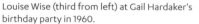

"The boys had baseball, and we roller-skated, played tag, or hop-scotch," says Gail. "Stamp collecting was huge. We'd go back to my house and sit out there at the picnic table and Mum would bring us lemonade. We'd have our stamp books out. A lot of people didn't even lock their doors. It wasn't like it is today; we never had parents driving us to school, even in grade one."

Both girls went to Windermere for high school. They ran track together occasionally, but because Gail was a year older, they drifted apart. "That's why it was kind of weird when Louise phoned me that day and asked me to come over. It was almost like a flash from the past," says Gail. "You know what it's like when you are a teenager; you're dating and working, and you don't see each other as much." But that day, Louise told Gail that her family was away on holidays and asked if she'd come over and visit. When Gail got there, Louise gave her friend a piece of birthday cake and showed her the new navy pant suit that her parents had bought for her seventeenth birthday. Louise planned to wear it to church that night.

Gail was surprised when Louise asked her about her boyfriend Al and confided in Gail that there was a man who was quite aggressive and had been bothering her at her flower-selling job. Louise gave her the impression that he was in his mid-twenties. Louise asked her friend to come back and spend the night, but Gail had a date and said that she couldn't. The girls left together, Gail to her house, Louise to a church service.

No one saw a man around Louise's house that night. Because there was no forced entry, police believe that he'd either followed her home from church or was already waiting for her at the house when she got back. Probably not knowing what else to do, it appeared that Louise let him in.

According to a newspaper story, Donald Menzies, an accountant for the florist company where Louise worked, said she had taken the Sunday shift off, but was scheduled to work on Monday. When she didn't turn up for her shift, Menzies said he didn't try to contact her because it was quite common for flowers girls to quit work without notice. He told a reporter that while "Louise was a very steady, very nice youngster," the turnover was extremely high among the girls. "If they don't turn up, we assume they're not coming to work that day or they don't want the job anymore."

Louise Wise (middle) in Gail Hardaker's backyard in 1966.

Courtesy Gail Hardaker

He told the reporter that he didn't know of any cases where girls were attacked while at work. "The odd idiot tries to make up to them while they're on the job, but I've never heard of one being physically molested," he said.

Slain Girl Found by Neighbour

A neighbour of the Wises who had been holidaying at Birch Bay with Louise's family returned to Vancouver early and promised that he would check in on Louise. When he couldn't reach her by phone, he went to the house on Thursday, four days after her disappearance, around 11:00 a.m.

He found Louise's body in the living-dining room. There were no signs of a struggle, but both the phones in the house had been ripped out of the wall. Police believe Louise was sexually attacked at knife point, and when that went wrong was choked unconscious and then stabbed four times in the chest with a butcher knife. The knife was still lodged in her when she was found.

After the murder, police asked Gail to write down everything she remembered about seeing Louise that night. There wasn't much Gail could tell them. Her notes say that a man—she never got his name—walked Louise home after her shift selling flowers outside the Broadway Liquor Store on the Friday before her murder. She didn't let him in, but he knew where she lived, and it's quite possible that he knew that her family was away.

Eve Lazarus photo, 2015

The Wise house on Lillooet Street, Vancouver.

"I know she was scared of him," says Gail. "She told me she didn't want to answer the phone. And, typical of a teenager, I said, 'Don't answer the phone.' That was my solution, not thinking that he would actually come to the house." Investigators took Gail's fingerprints so they could eliminate them from the ones in Louise's house. Gail's mother told her much later that police had followed her that summer from her home to her summer job at Woodward's Department Store because they were concerned that Louise might have identified her killer to Gail and that she might be in danger.

Diane (Fisher) Caleffi and Louise belonged to the same Bible group at Windermere Secondary and ate lunch together most days. "I remember our last day of school," she says. "We were having lunch, and we were so excited about graduation." Diane says that the summer of her friend's murder was the first time she experienced real fear. "You're seventeen years old and this happens to your friend and everybody is talking about how it happened. It was just so sad," she says. "Louise was almost nun-like; she had a peaceful, serene quality about her. She was a really nice, kind person, and she never had anything bad to say about anybody. She wanted to be a nurse. She would have been a great nurse." One month after Louise's murder, police still had no leads. "The investigation is plodding along," a police spokesman told a *Vancouver Sun* reporter. "There is nothing new to go on."

Then, in 1996, the Provincial Unsolved Homicide Unit launched with a

Geraldine Forster was shot to death at the train tracks near Renfrew Street and Grandview Highway in 1973.

mandate to reinvestigate cold cases. That year, the province had around 700 unsolved murders on its books. Brian Honeybourn was a detective sergeant with the unit, and he says that they were keen to reopen Louise Wise's murder case. He speculated that she was murdered by the same man who had killed Geraldine Forster less than two years later.

Girl Shot, Killed With Mountie's Gun at Grandview and Renfew

Nineteen-year-old Geraldine Forster was shot four times at Renfrew Street and Grandview Highway while returning home after walking her friend to the bus stop. She was shot with an RCMP-issued .38-calibre Smith and Wesson stolen from the Sechelt, BC, home of Constable Wayne Dingle.

Footprints found at the scene indicated that Geraldine had been running along the west side of Renfrew just before she was shot, and investigators thought that her attacker had jumped out from tall grass in a field next to the nearby railway tracks. It was possibly an attempted rape that turned to murder when she fled. Two bullets hit her in the legs from behind as she ran. The other two shots entered the front of her body. One bullet passed through her red nylon jacket and hit her just above the chest, the other hit her in her lower right shoulder.

Geraldine was originally from Fort St. John, but had been boarding with a family on East 14th Avenue for two years while she studied x-ray technology at the BC Institute of Technology. She'd recently graduated with honours and was about to complete her training at Vancouver General Hospital.

Her murder appeared to be random and baffled police for the next three years. Then, in April 1976, police on patrol in the False Creek area noticed a suspicious-looking character hanging around the Western Chemical Company on West 5th Avenue. The man identified himself as Dave Morris [name changed], aged thirty, who lived on Seaforth Drive in Vancouver's Renfrew area and worked in Surrey. When police searched his truck, they found a starting pistol and, under the driver's seat, Constable Dingle's stolen .38 service revolver. Dingle had been renting a house from friends of Morris, and Morris had been hired to do repairs there. Dingle testified that he had been away and didn't know his gun was missing until the day after the murder.

Morris had a previous conviction for rape, and it's possible he had met Geraldine in the neighbourhood. They both frequented Margaret Whistle's corner grocery store at Grandview and Renfrew, and the store owner told the court that Geraldine was often in the store, and because Morris was a regular, she stocked Sweet Caporal cigarettes especially for him. Morris was charged with the murder of Geraldine Forster, convicted, and sentenced to life imprisonment. While the *modus operandi* was different—Louise was stabbed and Geraldine shot—Honeybourn felt that the weapons were more a means of opportunity rather than a preferred method of killing. The two murders took place just several blocks apart. The problem for police was that there was nothing to link Geraldine's murder to Louise's. There were no witnesses, and there was no physical evidence. The only possible link would have come from DNA evidence, and that method became impossible after Honeybourn found that Louise's murder weapon, a butcher knife, was missing from the evidence room.

"It was a case we wanted to reopen. We wanted to take the knife apart and see if there was any possibility of DNA from the victim, and of course, we had no knife to take apart," he says. "Exhibits weren't cared for the way they are now. There was neglect and poor record-keeping. It could have been ten years later when somebody found the knife, but maybe the tag had fallen off it. In those days, what we would do is tie a paper tag to [the murder weapon], and God knows where it went." Without that crucial DNA evidence, the murder of Louise Wise remains unsolved.

Sources:
Province: July 16, 17, 1971; November 3, 1976
Vancouver Magazine: October 1977
Vancouver Sun: July 15, 16, 19, 20, 21; August 11, 1971; June 14, 1973; November 2, 3, 6, 9, 12, 1976

"A special RCMP squad has been formed to coordinate the investigation of serious crimes in the Vancouver area," the Globe and Mail *reported on July 22, 1976. "One of the first jobs of the six-man squad will be to check for similarities in the unsolved murders of at least twelve British Columbia women since January 1975."*

CHAPTER 13

From Langley to Nashville

I n 1974 Debbie and Vicky Roe were living the dream. The sister act—Debbie was twenty-two, and Vicky seventeen—had just returned from Nashville where they'd cut a country-and-western album called *Soft, Sweet and Country*. The record cover shows two beautiful young women—Vicky the brunette, Debbie the blonde—in a rural setting, dressed in flowing dresses and holding floppy hats. Life did indeed look sweet.

"We'd been singing together professionally for about four or five years," says Vicky. "We used to do talent contests around town, and we used to sing at the nightclubs before we could legally get in."

Vicky (left) and Debbie (right) on the album cover of *Soft, Sweet and Country* recorded in Nashville in 1973.

The Roes worked with George Calhoun, a local songwriter, and it was George who helped them get to Nashville. "George backed us up at talent contests. He really wanted to write a lot of the material and have us do the album in Nashville," says Vicky, adding that it was George who sent a demo tape to Cherish Records. The record label liked the demo, and Debbie and Vicky flew to Nashville to record.

Debbie and Vicky collaborated on a few of the songs. Their back-up musicians included some of the best talent in country music at the time—Bobbe Seymour, Steve Gibson, Buddy Emmons, and Charlie McCoy. McCoy had backed up artists such as Elvis Presley, Bob Dylan, and Johnny Cash and was inducted into the Country Music Hall of Fame in 2009. "It was big for us," says Vicky. "That's why it was just so tragic when it happened."

A family out for a walk in a rural area of Langley, BC, on February 22, 1975 found Debbie's body just off a road. She had been sexually assaulted, beaten, strangled, and left to drown in six inches (fifteen cm) of water. Coroner Doug Jack described the killing as "an enraged frustrated attack."

Link Sought in Two Deaths at Langley

Debbie's murder happened just two months after the body of Vancouver resident Barbara Ann LaRoque, also twenty-two years old, was found strangled and dumped in the bush north of Langley—only about a mile-and-a-half (2.4 km) from where Debbie's body was found. Barbara lived on East 3rd Avenue in Vancouver, and her death registration lists her as a restaurant waitress. According to a couple of articles in the major dailies, Barbara was a go-go dancer at a Vancouver nightclub called Syndicate City on Howe Street. One report said that a girl who may have been Barbara had been seen being dragged into a car outside the club where she worked. Another report said Syndicate City was owned by the same company as the OK Corral, where Debbie Roe had worked as a cocktail waitress.

Debbie grew up in the Fraser Valley and was one of five children. In 1975 her siblings ranged in age from five to twenty-three. Four months before she died, Debbie had moved out of her family's Aldergrove home to share an apartment in Langley with her friend Kym Neumann and Kym's dad. At eighteen, Kym was a few years younger than Debbie, but when they met they quickly became friends because of their shared interest in music. "Debbie did all the harmony, and Vicky did all the lead singing. I was just mesmerized by Debbie's voice," she says.

Debbie may have sung country, but she listened to rock. Her favourite bands were Bachman-Turner Overdrive and Chicago, and she loved Neil Young.

A popular, beautiful girl, she was a runner-up for Miss Surrey in 1973.

During the day, when work was available, Debbie was a flag girl for Traco Industries, a Vancouver construction company, but it wasn't enough to support her. Both Debbie and Kym worked as cocktail waitresses at the OK Corral in New Westminster, a bar that featured live country music acts.

Kym says Debbie wasn't home when she woke up on February 22, and she assumed that she'd stayed overnight with a friend. When Debbie still hadn't arrived home that afternoon, Kym started to worry. "Debbie didn't drink excessively or anything like that, but sometimes she spent the night with a friend because she was too tired to drive home," says Kym. "But if she spent the night at a girlfriend's house she was always home before noon, and she would ring the buzzer and say, 'Hi, it's me.'"

On the night Debbie died, she was driving home after finishing her shift at the OK Corral somewhere between 2:00 and 2:30 a.m. She stopped to get gas for her car and got something to eat at a Denny's restaurant on King George Highway.

Car Found Abandoned at Fry's Corner

Debbie's car, a three-year-old blue Chevrolet Nova, was found parked and locked on a desolate section of the Fraser Highway called Fry's Corner. Her body was found 4.6 miles (7.4 km) away in the 7700 block of 204th Street in Langley.

Police told the family that it was possible someone had followed Debbie because she disappeared so quickly after her car broke down. They said that the motor wouldn't start again, and Debbie began to hitchhike and was picked up by the person who killed her.

Her car was found pointing in the direction of Langley. "She would not have hitchhiked," says Kym. "It would have had to have been someone that she recognized for her to get in a car with some guy." Kym is also highly suspicious about the car breaking down. "That car was in really good shape. I used to drive it," she says. "I believe somebody did something to her car."

Debbie's long blonde wig was found by the road, and the family were told there were skin scrapings under her fingernails. When DNA came out as a forensics tool in the mid-1990s, the family were hopeful that finally they could catch Debbie's killer, but they were told that any items that may have carried DNA had been lost.

A week or so after her death, Kym and a boyfriend of Debbie's tried to trace the route she would have taken. They found the gas station where she'd gone to, and also the restaurant where she ate. "We used to stop there all the time and have something to eat after work," says Kym. The waiter told them that he remembered a man standing behind Debbie and that she looked flustered. Another witness told police that Debbie was having coffee with a man, but the witness never identified him.

New Evidence Prompts Second Look at Old Murder

Debbie's murder investigation was reinvestigated in 2003. "On a regular basis we revisit files to see if anything can resurface," Corporal Dale Carr told a reporter. "We are trying to generate tips." Carr said that police had received new information, but declined to say what it was. "We don't just shelve these things; we routinely bring them back to the forefront," he said. "There are a lot of times when people may not want to say something when they are twenty, but now that they are forty-eight years old, they feel differently."

Over the years, dozens of police officers have been assigned to Debbie's case. "Every couple of years there would be a new detective on it, and it's almost like starting from scratch again," says Vicky.

And there's always false hope too, she says. Police have looked at serial killers Clifford Olson and Ted Bundy as possible suspects. When Garry Handlen was charged in December 2014 in the 1975 murder of eleven-year-old Kathryn-Mary Herbert of Abbotsford and the 1978 murder of twelve-year-old Monica Jack of Merritt, the family thought they might finally have some closure.

Handlen, who would have been twenty-seven at the time of Debbie's murder, was well-known to police in the 1970s as a serial rapist. He was convicted of two brutal rapes in 1971 and 1978, and in 1979, he was sentenced to eighteen years in jail. It's not clear where Handlen was living in the mid-1970s, but in 1978 he was a resident of New Westminster. It appears there is no evidence to connect him with Debbie's death.

The family won't get closure until Debbie's murder is solved. The worst part, they say, is always wondering who did it. They've wondered about an older family friend who was infatuated with Debbie. They've wondered if it was a current or old boyfriend. They've even wondered if it was one of the two police officers who had sometimes stopped Debbie on her way home to ask her out. And they've wondered if it was a stranger who followed Debbie from the bar, someone she had met at Denny's, or someone they all knew.

"My dad started to get dementia in his last year. He would go to Langley with large amounts of money trying to pay people for information," says Vicky. "What an easy hit he was, and he died not knowing."

"If they ever had any suspects, they never told us," says Marianne Roe, Debbie's mother. "That's what has made me so mad. They've always kept it so close to their shirts. They told me I could get her file, and I sent away to get her file, and the file was just mainly things that I had said. Her murder file was nothing. They didn't give me anything."

"I was very disappointed—we all have been. There has been a lot of miscommunication," says Vicky. "Then, as the years go by, I guess we'll never know."

Vicky not only lost her sister, she lost a promising recording career. "I went on to make a various artists album with one of my cuts and a forty-five," she says. "Then I got married, and it wasn't really the same."

Marianne says the murder remains a mystery to the family. "The thing is, why? She was coming home from work. Her car wasn't working, and the next morning her car was found, and she was dead. Why? Who did it?"

Sources:
Langley Advance: February 28, 2003
Province: December 16, 1974; February 24, 1975; February 21, 2003
Vancouver Sun: December 14, 1974; February 24, 1975; July 9, 1976; December 2, 2014

*According to Neil Boyd, Director of the School of Criminology
at Simon Fraser University, in the 1970s murder rates were almost double
what they are today. "Part of it is demographics. In 1977 seventeen percent
of the Canadian population was made up of young men between the ages of
eighteen and thirty-five," he says. "Today, that group constitutes about ten percent
of the population, and we know they commit about seventy-five percent of
homicides in most countries and in every era of human history."*

CHAPTER 14

The Good Earth

In the fall of 1971, Bruce and Brenda Young rented out their North Vancouver house, packed their four kids and some belongings into a Volkswagen bus, and headed south. Bruce, a forty-four-year-old former reporter with the *Vancouver Sun* turned freelance writer, could work anywhere, and he wanted to write a book. Brenda, also a writer, would look after the family. The plan was to head to Mexico, learn some Spanish, gain an understanding of the culture, and source some local handicrafts with the idea of opening a shop on their return. The Youngs headed to the village of San Juan Cosala on the shores of Lake Chapala and rented a small house for one month. It had a couple of rooms and a courtyard, and they lived among the locals. "It was the best memory of my childhood," says their son Tom Young, who was eleven at the time.

Tom says he remembers his father driving about twenty of the local kids around in the old VW. The rent from their house financed most of their trip, but money was tight and mostly the family stayed in a tent trailer that they'd towed along for that purpose.

Where Bruce was loud and social, Brenda was a stabilizing factor in the family. "She really was one of the most caring people in that her entire life was to try to serve others and make everybody's life better," says Tom. "She cooked our dinners and tucked us in at night."

The family returned to North Vancouver the following year, bringing with them an assortment of clothing, crafts, and trinkets from Mexico and Guatemala. Brenda took over a leather goods store on Lower Lonsdale from its financially struggling owners and called it The Good Earth. She sold pottery, necklaces, jewellery, leather accessories, woven fabrics, hand-woven tapestries, and traditional Mayan clothing that the Youngs handpicked on buying trips.

Tom worked in the store occasionally, mostly after school and on weekends,

Vancouver Sun, January 8, 1976

Brenda Young was murdered in her store The Good Earth at the foot of Lonsdale Avenue in 1976.

and Bruce helped out from time to time, but it was Brenda who had the head for business. While the store was a family concern, the company was called Brenda Imports. By 1976 the small cedar-shake shop had a regular customer base, and she had turned The Good Earth into a thriving business.

Brenda was an attractive, petite woman with long, black curly hair, rosy cheeks, and a perpetual smile. She liked to dress in the clothes that she sourced from Guatemala and Mexico—long flowing denim skirts that she wore with big dangling earrings.

On the morning of January 7, 1976, Brenda opened the store an hour later than usual. The business was doing well enough that she and Bruce had decided to buy a second car for Brenda, and they'd met with a bank manager to take out a loan. Bruce dropped his wife off at the store where a neighbour was waiting for her with a bag of sticky buns.

The rest of the morning was uneventful. Brenda talked to a few regulars and served several customers. Bruce attempted to phone her just after 2:00 p.m., but there was no answer. He tried again a little later, and became increasingly worried when he phoned for a third time and still got no reply. "I felt that was not like her, and I wondered if she was not feeling well," Bruce later told Bernard Nash, the coroner at Brenda's inquest. "I told O'Day, 'Something is wrong.'"

Harry O'Day, their friend and the owner of the bookstore next door, was having a quiet day. There was only one customer in O'Day's store when Bruce phoned, and Harry's friend Carl Edward Paine, a folk singer who lived in East Vancouver, had dropped by to give Harry a late Christmas present. Harry tried the front door of Brenda's store and found it locked, but the lights were still on. He reported back to Bruce. Bruce asked them to break in through the bookstore and stayed on the phone.

Harry and Carl went to the back of the bookstore where there was a thin plywood board covering a hole that separated the two stores. They pried open enough of the panelling to gain access to a changing room. Carl opened the curtain and was the first to see Brenda. "I was stunned for about a minute, but it seemed like a lifetime," Carl later testified at the inquest. "I went back to the plywood and said, 'Don't go in, Harry, it's heavy!'"

"Carl told me what had happened. I didn't want to look—she was such a nice person," Harry told a reporter. "It was a senseless killing. I feel guilty about it. I was there right next door and never heard a scream or noticed anything wrong." Harry said later that he could not remember seeing any customers coming or going from Brenda's boutique and didn't hear any noise. He told a reporter that he knew her quite well. "She was not a bizarre character or far-out. Brenda, for God's sake, why pick on her?"

Then Carl and Harry had to give the terrible news to Bruce—that Brenda had been stabbed, strangled, and left at the back of her store. Harry said, "They were good neighbours. I liked them very much. Poor little woman, she didn't deserve anything like that. She was really nice."

Murder Puzzles Police

Brenda was well-known and much loved in North Vancouver's Deep Cove neighbourhood and the adjoining Dollarton area where they lived. Neighbours described her as a beautiful person; warm, generous, and kind. She had written a weekly column for the *North Shore Citizen* for several years that covered day-to-day activities of importance to the tight-knit community. "She was active in many things in the Deep Cove area," said her editor Ralph Hall. "She was outstanding in community work."

The Brenda Young murder was the last case Staff Sergeant Fred Bodnaruk worked on before his retirement in July 1976, after twenty-six years on the job. He was in charge of the major crimes detail for North Vancouver, and he also led the original unsolved homicides section, which travelled province-wide. Bodnaruk was the first RCMP officer at Brenda's murder scene and remembers the case clearly four decades later. "It was sad as hell because we put a terrific effort into solving her murder and we really didn't want to get defeated," he says. "It was one of these very unfortunate no-break situations."

Bodnaruk said he found Brenda lying face down in a pool of blood. She had been gagged with a cloth, but it was untied, and there were no signs of a struggle. "To our horror, we walked in and saw her body lying there. There was blood everywhere. A quick glance showed she was slashed and stabbed in the neck—there was a pretty wide slash around her throat."

Brenda had four cuts across the front of her neck, but the blood loss from the lacerations wasn't the principal cause of death. Rather, an autopsy revealed that death "was due to strangulation of the neck." The marks on her neck, as well as other signs—a rash on her face and around her eyelids—indicated strangulation probably by a cord or wire.

Because Brenda had been gagged but not tied up, Bodnaruk thought that either there were two people involved or the murderer had threatened her with the knife and told her she would be okay as long as she didn't make any noise. Although she wasn't sexually assaulted, Bodnaruk didn't rule that out as a motive for her murder. "Maybe rape was intended because she was found in the hallway away from the main store and where people couldn't see in," he says. "She was a strong woman, and she'd fight back. He might have strangled her to keep her quiet. If he got his knife out, and suppose he was a sadist, strangling her may not have been enough."

Police searched through the store, looking for the murder weapon. They discovered that Brenda had been making out an invoice for a customer just before she died. Bodnaruk thinks it was likely for her murderer.

Public Asked to Help Catch Killer
"We spent a considerable time at the scene going back and forth, and then we

put out a request for information for anyone to come forward that might have seen someone walk into the store," Bodnaruk says.

A twenty-five-year-old woman contacted police and said that she and her boyfriend were in The Good Earth shortly after 1:00 p.m. on the day of the murder. Brenda greeted them, but was serving a man who was already browsing in the store. Brenda didn't seem to know the man. The woman, who said she was "fearful for her safety," did not have her name released. She said that the man turned his back to her and she didn't get a look at his face. "He wasn't interested in the blouses and seemed uneasy," she said. "When I got outside of the shop I told my boyfriend that he seemed strange." The witness said she had shopped in Brenda's store about a dozen times in the previous year and knew her to be "pleasant and helpful." The witness stayed in the store for about ten minutes. She said she never saw the man's face and would not recognize him if she saw him again, but she was able to tell police that he was over six feet tall, in good physical condition, and between thirty and thirty-five. She also noticed that he was clean shaven with medium-brown, collar-length hair and was well-dressed in brown pants and a hip-length, light-brown leather jacket.

"In my professional opinion, that would have been the murderer," says Bodnaruk. "He was most timely on the scene. If he was a stranger, he wouldn't worry so much about being recognized. Because many times you go up and down the street and describe a person and people will say, 'Well that sounds

Vancouver Sun, January 8, 1976

The interior of The Good Earth store where Brenda Young's body was found.

like so and so.'" Bodnaruk thought the murderer may have been to the boutique before. He knew where to kill her and place the body where it wouldn't be seen in the back of the store, and there was nothing disturbed in the shop.

When another witness came forward and told police that she had tried to enter the store and found it locked, they narrowed Brenda's time of death to between 1:35 and 2:15 p.m. No one saw a blood-soaked man fleeing the crime scene, and no one reported seeing a disturbed individual around the time of her death. Bodnaruk believes this was likely because the murderer escaped through the back lane. The strip of Lower Lonsdale where The Good Earth was located was frequented by young transients, but except for the nearby Olympic Hotel, it was generally a quiet area.

Murder Stirs Unrest on Lower Lonsdale

The murder shocked the community. "That is something that is supposed to happen in New York or Philadelphia," Angela McQuannie of the Moodyville Landing Plant Shop told a reporter from the *North Shore News* a few days later. "The murderer must have been a lunatic." McQuannie said she had added two locks to her doors and was never alone in her store. "There are always two of us," she said. "It looks like Fort Knox in here."

The RCMP put twelve investigators onto the case, who checked and eliminated more than forty individuals. They searched the entire area of Lower Lonsdale with tracker dogs, but the killer hadn't left clothing or a murder weapon behind, and the dogs couldn't pick up a scent. "If he had left a jacket, man, we would have had him," says Bodnaruk. "There was no knife found at the scene. He wouldn't need much of a knife. A jack knife is a horrific killer, and a lot of people carry knives for various reasons."

Bodnaruk thought he'd finally got a break when they were checking drycleaners in the area. "We found one jacket that fit the description that was in for cleaning and we thought, 'Holy God, was he dumb enough to do that?' Turned out he wasn't."

Police ruled out robbery as a motive. No money was missing from the cash drawer, and as Bodnaruk pointed out, it wasn't the sort of store that you would target for a robbery.

Brenda's murder was so rapid and risky that it smacked of professionalism, says the former RCMP officer. He thought that with the Youngs' connection to Mexico and Central America, the murder could have been part of a drug connection gone wrong. "She wasn't a drug user, but she could have been a mule," he says. "And while we had a number of suspects, we didn't have DNA [testing] back then. She was running back and forth to Mexico, and I thought she might have shortchanged somebody and pissed somebody off."

While a professional hit-man or a serial killer seems absurd in sleepy North Vancouver, Bodnaruk says that Vancouver was known as the drug capital of Canada—a title that the city had worn since Danny Brent's murder in 1954. Most of the professional hits were by gun or club, and disposal was usually by dumping the body in the bush, he said.

"The store was kind of a hippie place, and she used to buy pretty outlandish clothes with lots of seams in them. We seized a whole bunch of clothes and had the ident man go over them," he says. "We did a massive search through all the clothing in the store looking for drug traces or packages. We tried to trace communications—who she phoned, her contacts—but we never found anything." They made international inquiries to see if there was a Mexican connection with whom she may have fallen out. "But the volume of business that she conducted was so nominal that even if she cheated somebody out of a payment they wouldn't use a hit man," Bodnaruk says.

Brenda was a vibrant and attractive woman, and while there was no evidence that she was seeing anyone outside her marriage, police looked at the possibility of a rejected would-be lover. Nothing turned up. "Just the way she was attacked and with such fury—we tried to figure out, why her?" says Bodnaruk. "She wasn't a flirt, but they did have lots of friends and partied pretty hard, so we thought maybe someone put the make on her and got rejected, but we couldn't find anyone like that."

Husband Questioned in North Van Murder

When inquiries failed to turn up a robbery, drug connection, or spurned lover, investigators turned their attention to Bruce Young. Bruce agreed to a polygraph and passed, and police tapped his phone. There was nothing to connect him to his wife's murder.

Bodnaruk interviewed Bruce and didn't believe he'd be able to commit an act of such violence. "I hope I am right, but I'll tell you one thing, if he had murdered her, he would have had to hire somebody," says Bodnaruk. "He was kind of a milquetoast guy."

Frustrated and with no leads, police brought in a clairvoyant who was visiting from England to help them solve the murder. According to Bodnaruk, while working with a clairvoyant wasn't common, it wasn't unheard of either, and the clairvoyant had helped British police on several occasions. "I said, 'What have we got to lose?'" Bodnaruk says. "You can't discount these people completely, and you just never know when fate will give you a break. You're playing this guessing game, because most investigation is guessing and probing and thinking based on a few leads." In this case, however, the clairvoyant was unable to help.

Early in 2015 Corporal Gord Reid of the North Vancouver RCMP detachment thought he finally had a break in the case via a lead through ViCLAS (Violent Crime Linkage Analysis System)—a database that helps investigators link major crimes. "I felt that I had a reasonably viable suspect on the Brenda Young homicide," says Reid. "I was about to fly far away to interview the man in prison where he was doing time for another fairly similar murder, but unfortunately the man died before I could get there." Reid says there was no DNA evidence from the 1976 crime scene to check against the suspect's.

Brenda's murder devastated her family, especially her four children, Heather, Tom, Jennifer, and ten-year-old Sheila. "Back in the 1970s, there were no counsellors," says Tom, who was sixteen at the time of his mother's murder. "You were just on your own. That was the very worst aspect of it. When she died, it caused a ripple in the community that never stopped."

Brenda was the centre of the family, and after she died, Bruce started drinking heavily. He was estranged from his Scottish parents, who lived in Victoria, as well as his brother Michael Young, a successful lawyer who was, at the time of Brenda's murder, the mayor of Victoria. The problem for the Young children was that Bruce refused all offers of help. "He would not allow any help, although he clearly needed it," says Tom. "He was destroyed by it for the rest of his life." Bruce died from lung cancer at age sixty-four.

In 1979 Bruce self-published a book called *Hotel California*, in which he refers to the family's travels south and to his wife's murder.

> The murder served to rekindle my interest in writing. In fact it was my immediate response as I sought to put my shattered life back together again. I went back to The Good Earth armed with my typewriter, my notes and the diaries Brenda had written during our travels. That return to the store was also a traumatic experience; logic said we should have given up the enterprise. After all it had nothing more to offer us than a daily reminder of a dreadful event. Offsetting this was the stark economic fact that all our resources were invested in the business. Correctly, or incorrectly, I decided that I must keep the flag flying over The Good Earth.

Bruce may have decided to keep the store, but he was running it into the ground. Tom dropped out in the middle of grade twelve to take over the business. His father returned to Mexico to finish his book. "It was a terrible time," says Tom. "People would come in and ask about Mum's murder. They'd ask if we were selling drugs. They were really rude."

Tom ran The Good Earth at that Lonsdale Street location until the early 1990s. He is still in the retail clothing business. The Lonsdale Street store survived until 2013 when it and other surrounding retail shops were replaced by a five-storey mixed-use development called the Versatile Building.

Sources:
North Shore Citizen: January 14, 28; February 11, 1970; January 9; June 30, 1976
North Shore News: January 14, 28, 1976
Province: January 8, 9, 10, 12, 13, 20; February 21, 1976
Vancouver Sun: January 9, 10, 12, 20; February 21, 22; March 13, 1976
Young, Bruce. *Hotel California*. The Good Earth, 1979.

Rhona Duncan's murder remains one of North Vancouver's seventeen
unsolved cases dating back to 1964. After 2003 new investigations were
transferred to IHIT—the RCMP's Integrated Homicide Investigation Team,
the largest homicide unit in Canada. IHIT serves twenty-nine RCMP
communities and three municipal police departments.

CHAPTER 15

Sweet Sixteen

I t was July 16, 1976, the night of Margaret Peters' [name changed] seventeenth birthday party. Margaret was allowed to invite twenty friends to share a quiet celebration with her parents, brothers, and sisters in their North Vancouver home.

Margaret was on the student council at Carson Graham Secondary School and had just finished grade eleven along with more than 600 other students who came from several feeder schools including Balmoral, Sutherland, and Hamilton. Margaret's guest list was comprised almost entirely of friends she'd known at Balmoral. A few guests brought dates from other schools.

Although Shawn Mapoles went to Delbrook Senior Secondary School, he knew Margaret from Balmoral, and he'd brought Rhona Duncan to the party that night. Shawn and Rhona had been on several dates before the night of the party, and Shawn's friend Owen Parry was dating Rhona's friend Marion Bogues.

It wasn't long before Margaret's quiet celebration started to get out of control. Dozens of North Vancouver teenagers who were hanging out at Ambleside Beach and Mahon Park heard about a house party and crashed the East Queens Road house. Underage teens poured through the front door, armed with booze. Others scrambled over the back fence, through the neighbour's yard. A plate that one of the Peters had brought back from an overseas trip was knocked off the wall and smashed, drinks were spilled on the carpet, and teens perched themselves on the stereo system and soon overran the house. The Peters called the police. "It was supposed to be a celebratory night for me, and it turned out to be a really horrible mess and something I'll never forget," says Margaret. "It was one of those parties where word gets around and everybody comes. I didn't know half the people." When the police arrived sometime after midnight, the party crashers scattered.

As bad as the mess in the house appeared, it was nothing compared to the news that came the next day. Margaret got a phone call from a friend who said that a girl from her school who had been at her party just hours before was dead.

Eve Lazarus photo, 2015

The East Queens Road house and the scene of the party on July 16, 1976.

Girl Slain on Street Near Home

Shawn, Rhona, Marion, and Owen left the Peters home around 1:00 a.m. It was a warm summer night, and they took their time walking in the direction of all four of their homes. They stopped at the municipal hall on West Queens. Owen and Shawn lived up the hill, and Rhona and Marion lived in the Hamilton area. The girls wanted to be by themselves to talk about the night; it was an easy walk down Jones Avenue.

"Normally, I would walk a woman home, but Rhona didn't want me to walk her home that night," says Shawn. "Marion was her best friend, and she was a very big and powerful woman. She said, 'Don't worry about it. I'll take care of her.' She lived just a couple of blocks away." Marion, who was nicknamed "the Train," played on Carson Graham's girl's football team. Rhona and Marion stopped and talked for a while and then parted company near Marion's home at the corner of Larson Road and Wolfe Street.

Rhona disappeared into the darkness of Larson Road, turned south on Bewicke Avenue, and was at the intersection at West 15th, the quiet residential street where she lived, when someone stopped her. She was about 100 feet (30.5 m) from a street light, and in sight of the safety of her home.

Eve Lazarus photo, 2015

The lane where Rhona was found on 15th Avenue and Bewicke Avenue in North Vancouver.

Around 3:00 a.m., Joyce Holzermayr, a neighbour of the Duncans, woke from a deep sleep. She thought she heard a man and a woman arguing on the street near the house and woke her husband William, asking him to go out and investigate. William Holzermayr got out of bed and shouted, "What's going on here?" The arguing stopped and all was quiet. Holzermayr later recalled that it sounded "more or less like a lovers' quarrel," but when he looked out, he could see nothing, and it was common to hear young people's voices late at night on the weekends, he said. Thinking nothing of it, he went back to bed and fell asleep. None of the other neighbours reported seeing or hearing anything.

By 4:00 a.m. Rhona was dead. She had been raped and strangled.

The next morning, Hondrie Werbowski was on her way to work when she saw Rhona's body lying in the tall grass in front of a garage in a lane off Bewicke. "I was walking along, and all of a sudden I could see an arm," Hondrie later told a reporter. "The sun was shining on something—I guess it was the blonde hair. I didn't want to see," she said. "I just didn't want to see what it was."

Hondrie called to William and Joyce Holzermayr, the owners of the corner house, and Joyce walked up to the body and grabbed her arm. "It's a girl," she told the others. She saw that Rhona had been stripped naked from the waist down. Police secured the murder scene and the body was taken to the morgue.

Eve Lazarus photo, 2015

The Duncan house on West 15th Street, North Vancouver.

Rhona's mother and father, Roy and Frederic Duncan, woke the next morning to find that their daughter had not come home that night. Hearing a commotion outside, they went to see what was happening only to receive the heartbreaking news that the girl who was found in the lane was most likely Rhona.

Middle-class Neighbourhood
The Duncans had lived in their 1912 Arts and Crafts heritage house on West 15th Avenue since 1967. The upper-middle-class neighbourhood backed onto a private woodland setting at the end of a cul-de-sac and was comprised of established houses and long-time neighbours.

A chartered accountant from Ireland, Frederic Duncan was the secretary/controller at Pacific Press when they moved to West 15th Avenue, and in 1975 he had taken a job as vice-president for Jones Tent and Awning in Vancouver. Rhona was the eldest of four girls in a family that neighbours described as "close." They said Rhona was a "lovely, pretty girl."

"I watched them grow up," Thelma Riddell, who lived across the street from the Duncan's, told a newspaper reporter after the murder. "Four lovely little girls. They were always in and out of the yard, playing up and down the street. I can't believe how something like that could happen to a girl like that.

It's a very quiet neighbourhood with a dead-end street. She was so near home, you know. It's a terrible shock to everyone."

Hondrie Werbowski, the unfortunate neighbour who found Rhona's body, told a reporter that she had lived down the street from the Duncans for the past six years. She described Rhona as a "typical teenager—a nice girl, a popular girl" who was a student at Carson Graham secondary.

Teresa (Zwanski) Shannon went to Carson Graham and raised her own children in North Vancouver. Nearly four decades later, the unsolved murder still haunts her. While she didn't know Rhona or her group of friends outside of school, she and Rhona shared the same French class. Teresa remembers Rhona as a quiet girl with dark-blonde hair. "I don't know if she was shy, but I remember she was quiet in the classroom. She was not one who would attract attention to herself," she says. "She was a nice-looking girl, just your average kid."

Shawn Mapoles found out about his girlfriend's murder when his friend Owen called him the next morning. The shocked teens went to Marion's house and tried to figure out what had happened and what they could have done differently. Rhona, he says, was a small girl, about five-foot-four, thin, who weighed about 110 pounds (50 kg). "She was a very down-to-earth basic person, very cute, very stable," he says.

When Shawn arrived home later that morning, there was a police car outside his door. RCMP had bagged and taken away the clothes he'd worn the night before. He was interviewed that night. Shawn took a polygraph and offered to help in any way possible. Not only was he innocent, he desperately wanted to find Rhona's murderer. He thought that if he'd just pushed Rhona a bit harder on the night of the party and walked her home, she would still be alive. "I felt guilty," says Shawn. "I had always walked my girlfriend home, made sure she got in safely, and I didn't that night, and see how things turned out."

Police questioned Shawn on Rhona's insistence on walking home

Rhona Duncan in the Carson Graham Secondary School yearbook, 1976.

Courtesy Teresa Shannon

with Marion and speculated that perhaps she had been meeting someone later that night. It seemed more likely that the murderer had attended the party and followed the girls, or had seen the girls walking home and targeted Rhona—a crime of opportunity.

As Sergeant Mel Tait, who headed up the investigation for the RCMP, told a reporter: "You can go a couple of ways on this one. Was it someone who knew her who she was going to meet? Or was it just some freak who happened to see her walking home alone? We can't be sure."

Police asked Shawn if he remembered anyone paying a lot of attention to Rhona at the party. He told them that while he knew a lot of the kids there that night, he couldn't remember anything that seemed strange or out of place. "We were just getting to know each other, so I was focussing my attention on Rhona, not on my surroundings," he says.

Was Rhona's Killer at the Party?

Sue Penner [name changed] thinks the killer could have been at Margaret Peters' party. The sixteen-year-old Argyle Secondary student had crashed the party with her boyfriend and their friends, and she remembers talking to Rhona in the living room. She says her attention was drawn to an older guy—maybe twenty or twenty-one—who was a friend of her boyfriend's older brother and didn't seem to fit in with the largely teenaged crowd.

After the police closed down the party, she left with her group of friends. She remembers the older boy from the party trailing behind them. Later she says she saw Rhona and another girl walking ahead of them, and then Rhona

Courtesy Gord Curl

A group of grade-eleven Carson Graham students. Rhona Duncan farthest left in the front row.

walking down Larson Road alone. "I can still remember how dark that road was, and she began to run. What idiots we were letting her go alone in the dark," says Sue.

Sue says that her mother was away, and she was staying with her grandfather that night. He was angry with her for coming home so late, but he never told her mother and neither did Sue. "I did call the police station a few days after and left a message that we had been walking along with Rhona, and I would tell them any details, but nobody called me back," she says. "I never even told my husband about this. I guess I felt guilty. I always thought they would be able to find the person."

Margaret Peters also feels some guilt. Police interviewed the family the next day, trying to come up with a guest list for the party. But as Margaret told them, she didn't know most of the people who were there. "The police demanded a guest list, and I felt like they were blaming me," she says. "And even though I didn't know Rhona that well, it still bothers me. Maybe if she hadn't been at my party this might not have happened. Or if I'd been able to remember something more, would they have been able to solve it?"

Assault Linked to Murder

Police were also investigating a connection between Rhona's death and an attempted assault on a woman in North Vancouver a few days before, as well as an attempted abduction of a sixteen-year-old girl just hours before the attack on Rhona.

At around midnight, a man had grabbed a girl from behind in an attempt to force her into his car near 3rd Street and St. Andrews Avenue. According to police, he clamped a hand over her mouth. The girl freed herself by biting the man's hand and then screaming. He released her and then sped off in a late model two-door red car with a white interior and a black hardtop. She described him as a thirty-year-old male, about six feet tall, weighing between 150 and 170 pounds (68 and 77 kg) with a slim build and a pointy chin. His blond hair was neat, and police thought it might have been a wig. RCMP Constable Smith speculated to a reporter that it was possible that "he did not get what he was after and so continued to cruise the streets."

Just a few days before Rhona's murder, a twenty-seven-year-old North Vancouver woman was assaulted at 21st Street and Mahon Avenue shortly after getting off a bus around midnight. Police say her assailant opened his pants, made an obscene suggestion, knocked her to the ground, and tried to pull down her underwear. As he tried to jump on her she pushed him away, kicked him, and screamed. She told police that her attacker pleaded with her, "Don't scream—please don't scream." When a light came on at one of the houses on the street, he ran off.

The woman told a reporter that even though she had screamed in that quiet residential area, no one had bothered to come to her assistance. The next day, she said, she called on the neighbours whose homes bordered the narrow grassy strip where she was attacked to ask why they didn't respond to her screams.

"All they could say was, 'We're sorry.'" The woman said police told her that she would have had a better chance of attracting attention if she had screamed "fire," because that cry would have more strongly appealed to the homeowners' self-interest.

She described her attacker as in his early twenties with a slim build, around five-foot-ten and weighing 150 pounds (68 kg). He had dark-brown, shoulder-length hair and a light-brown moustache, and he was wearing jeans and a jean jacket. The description was similar to one given of a young man seen near Wolfe Street and Larson Road around the time of Rhona's death. Police felt he may have lived in that area.

Special Squad Studies Killings for Similarities

After interviewing more than forty people, and with no suspects, on July 22, five days after the murder, the RCMP announced that they had formed a special squad to coordinate the investigation of several serious crimes around the province. Police were searching for a serial killer. The six-man squad formed under Sergeant Arnold Nyland would check for similarities in the unsolved sex slayings of at least twelve women since January 1975.

One murder in particular caught their attention. Sixteen-year-old Brenda Kercher of Langley had been raped and killed by a blow to the head on July 3, just two weeks before Rhona's death. Both girls were at parties immediately prior to their murders, but a check of the guest lists didn't reveal any common connections with this or the other murders. Brenda Kercher's murder was eventually solved and her killer sent to jail.

Police prepared a list of 172 males that included all of Rhona's friends and acquaintances and all the men who were in the area at the time of the murder and had a past history of sexual assault. They conducted numerous polygraph examinations and interviewed dozens of suspects but remained stumped.

Shawn Mapoles, who is now an accountant with the federal government and still lives in North Vancouver, says police have contacted him three times over the last four decades, and he says that Rhona's file has been reinvestigated twice that he is aware of. "The first time they called a couple of us in and reinterviewed us to see if anything jogged [our memories]," he says. "They were looking at the case and confirming statements and that type of thing, and the second time they had DNA evidence and wanted to get voluntarily samples from people." That was in 1998, when advances in DNA technology made it possible for police to obtain a DNA profile of Rhona's attacker from exhibits seized during the investigation. Some of the suspects were never found, some had died, and a few refused to cooperate.

Under current law, police cannot get a DNA warrant to rule out suspects even in a murder case. "Police can only take DNA voluntarily, and I know there were a few people who strongly objected," says Shawn. "What their motives were for doing that, I don't know." Shawn and other friends who attended Margaret's party that night have met several times over the years to discuss the case. They believe the murderer may have been someone at the party with them.

Given that sexual predators are highly likely to reoffend and that several of the suspects in the Rhona Duncan investigation had criminal pasts that included sexual attacks on women, it's not surprising that they would refuse to hand over their DNA.

But police seem no closer to solving Rhona's murder than they were four decades ago. They've interviewed hundreds of witnesses and possible suspects, performed polygraphs on the higher priority suspects, and tested DNA. The case remains boxed up inside the cold file room, where every now and then it's taken out, dusted off, and re-examined.

In 2003 Sergeant Gerry Webb told North Vancouver's *Outlook* newspaper that more than two-thirds of the subjects had been cleared through the DNA comparison. New to the case at that time, Webb had dug through the eight boxes of evidence that included tip sheets, police officers' notes, crime-scene photographs, and an autopsy report.

Webb told the reporter that the men they viewed as suspects would continue to be contacted to voluntarily come to the North Vancouver RCMP detachment for a DNA test; if the DNA is not a match, the samples will be destroyed, he said. "The present focus of the investigation is to continue with DNA collection from outstanding suspects," said Webb.

Sources:
Globe and Mail: July 22, 1976
North Shore Citizen: July 21, 28, 1976
North Shore Outlook: February 27, 2003; March 9, 2006
Province: July 19, 20, 1976; February 25, 2007
Vancouver Sun: July 19, 20, 23, 30, 1976

A story by the Globe and Mail *on March 13, 1985, noted that
some Vancouver gangs had up to eighty members, usually aged between
fifteen and twenty-five: "Armed with guns, baseball bats, iron bars,
machetes, cleavers and knives, they have been terrorizing the
Vancouver east side and its 100,000 residents for months."*

CHAPTER 16

On the Edge of Chinatown

At the start of 1985, things looked good for Jimmy Ming. At twenty-nine, he was the popular manager of the Yangtse Kitchen, the family restaurant that he had helped build from three tables on Denman Street into a thriving Robson Street business.

The family was originally from Taiwan and had settled in Vancouver's Strathcona neighbourhood in the early 1970s. Jimmy and his three brothers graduated from King George Secondary School. He married Lily Hsiuo, and by 1985 they had two small children, Jason, six, and Elisa, five, and lived around the corner from the East Georgia Street house owned by his parents.

Jimmy typically worked twelve- to fifteen-hour days at the Yangtse Kitchen on Robson near Nicola Street. Lily learned English at night school, took care of the children, and worked in the restaurant one day a week. Everything seemed to be working out for the family. But by the end of January, Jimmy and Lily had been kidnapped from their home, the restaurant was closed, and the rest of the Ming family lived in fear for their own lives.

On Saturday, January 19, the Ming family was at the Fairyland Restaurant on Fraser Street celebrating the wedding of Jimmy's younger brother John to a Vietnamese woman. The celebration hadn't gone smoothly. A fight broke out, and onlookers estimated later that it involved many of the 300 mainly Vietnamese guests. Jimmy was tired, and he and Lily left for their Princess Street home around 10:30 p.m. The children spent the night with their grandparents.

Sometime after midnight, in the early hours of January 20, an unknown number of kidnappers approached the Ming house from the laneway, smashed a basement window, entered, and abducted the couple.

The kidnapping was discovered that afternoon, when Jimmy's father, Ping Chang Ming, received a ransom note asking for $700,000. When translated into English, the note read: "You have a good family. You have a good business. We don't have anything. We have a lot of brothers and you won't catch us all.

Eve Lazarus photo, 2015

The house on Princess Avenue, where the Mings were abducted in January 1985.

We are even in the United States. You will not be the last. There will be other restaurants." Ping Chang Ming called police.

The kidnapping baffled friends and neighbours of the Mings, who couldn't understand why the young couple were targeted. While the Ming family owned property and the restaurant was doing well, they were far from rich. Jimmy drove an old station wagon, and the home they'd owned for three years on the edge of Chinatown was nice but modest. "They owned a restaurant where they worked sixteen hours a day," one friend told a reporter. "They were not getting rich on that income. If somebody was after a big ransom, these were not the right people to kidnap." They speculated that the kidnapping might have started with a robbery. The Mings, they said, may have been targeted because they were about to leave on holiday for Taiwan and may have had a large sum of cash handy in anticipation of the trip.

Friends told reporters that the Mings employed some "boat people"—refugees from Vietnam—at the restaurant and conjectured that a Vietnamese youth gang may have been responsible.

Asian Gangs Linked to Kidnapping

Constable Bob Cooper, a member of the Vancouver Police Department's Asian gang squad, told reporters that gangs recruited youth in schools. While the kids were typically the ones ordered to do the shooting because of the lighter sentences that they'd receive if caught, they were the lowest echelon on the organized crime ladder.

Terry Gould was a substitute teacher at Britannia Secondary School in East Vancouver two years after the Ming case hit the front pages. In his book *Paper Fan: The Hunt for Triad Gangster Steven Wong*, he writes that it was widely known to neighbourhood kids that Chinese businesses near the school were paying protection money, and those who refused were punished. He says that it was the Asian crime squad's suspicion that the murder of Jimmy and Lily Ming may have been linked to problems that Jimmy's father, Ping Chang Ming, was having with the Triads back in Taiwan. Rumours in the Asian underworld, he said, indicated that the Viet Ching gang—named after a slang term used to refer to Vietnamese of Chinese descent—were hired to kill the Mings as retribution, and the $700,000 ransom was merely an extra windfall.

Seven weeks after they went missing, the bodies of the Mings were found at the bottom of an embankment in dense bush off the Squamish Highway north of Vancouver between Porteau Cove and Lions Bay. An autopsy showed that the Mings were murdered shortly after they were abducted from their house. They had been strangled.

According to the *Squamish Times*, the highway had become a popular location to dump bodies. Over the previous decade, ten bodies had been found between Horseshoe Bay and Squamish.

Chinese Ads Used in Kidnapping

Somehow, the kidnappers found out that Ping Chang Ming had talked to police, and they sent a letter demanding an apology. The letter prompted a series of messages in local Chinese newspapers apologizing for angering the kidnappers and pleading for the lives of the missing Mings.

The first ad ran on February 13, and then every day for a week in both the *Chinese Times* and the *Chinese Voice*. When translated from Chinese, it read: "Mr Chin: Last time I was wrong. Please forgive me. We will do according to your wish. You demand too much. I have the heart but not the strength. Hope you will reconsider."

On March 3, forty-two days had passed since Ping Chang had last spoken to his son and daughter-in-law. He ran more ads pleading with the kidnappers for proof that the couple was still alive and telling of the problems he was having in raising the ransom money.

"Mr Wong," read the translated ad. "Your demand is acceptable. I really want to cooperate with you deep down in my heart. You make the plans for what you want me to do. But without a chance to talk to you, it's difficult. Please think. In the newspapers, it's really hard to explain. I am willing to give you the money, but understand my hardship. Asking the bank for money, you have to have a good reason. The house is already mortgaged, but that's not enough. Please, can I personally speak to my son and his wife? Get them individually to write a letter so I can see. Please be kind and think it over." The letter was signed by Mr Yang, the code name demanded by the kidnappers. Ming didn't hear from them again.

Police Superintendent Ray McNeney, who was in charge of the investigation, called the demand for an apology "psychological pressure." He said, "The demands were certainly unrealistic and exorbitant. It was something the family couldn't come up with." McNeney said that the kidnappers telephoned the father once from Victoria and mailed four notes to the restaurant.

"We never reached the stage where the directions said, 'Do something at such and such a time,'" McNeney told reporters. "Our hope from day one was that the couple was still alive because of the number of notes. We felt we had a chance to negotiate, and that the family had a chance to verify they were still alive."

Ming Abductors Threaten to Kill Brothers "One by One"

Gim Huey, vice-president of the Chinese Benevolent Association of Canada in Vancouver, told a reporter that he had seen all the ransom notes. One note threatened other members of the Ming family, said Huey. It read: "If you want to see your sons again, you'll come up with the money, or else eventually your sons will be killed one by one." The notes were written in Chinese by someone with a low level of education. "The language would seem to indicate that. They used a lot of slang-type words," he said. The content of the notes led police to suspect that the kidnapping was the work of one of the Asian youth gangs terrorizing East Vancouver.

A large influx of Vietnamese refugees entered Canada in the early 1980s. With no English, little education, few meaningful career prospects, and no family to support them, the young people among these refugees were perfect recruits for the Asian gangs.

Dr Robert Gordon, professor of criminology at Simon Fraser University, studies Asian gangs. He believes that the Mings were victims of a home invasion that went badly. Kidnappings are messy and require a great deal of organization. More likely, he says, the criminals saw an opportunity to make money from a ransom and decided to try to extort the family after the couple was already dead. "One theory for the Mings' killings was that it was a bunch of entrepreneurs who knew of them, knew of their movements, thought there was money in the house, thought there might have been money in the business, and went ahead and kidnapped them and said, 'Fork over, or we will kill you,'" says Gordon. "These organizations are in it for the money, and whatever will yield easy and untraceable cash is a fair target. There's not a huge amount of faith in financial institutions among Chinese, so a lot of assets would have been held in cash or gold."

Gangs Gunning for Each Other in Growing War

In 1985, the year the Mings were murdered, the Vancouver Police Department reported that eight gangs of Asian youths, with about 100 "hard-core" members in total, were involved in illegal activities that ranged from robbery and extortion to drug-dealing, pimping, and gambling. In response, the police department established an Asian crime squad to investigate gang activity and try to curtail it. The Lotus, Red Eagles, and Viet Ching gangs were identified as the most criminally active. The Viet Ching became active in Vancouver around 1982. The gang was extremely aggressive in their attempts to take over traditional Chinatown rackets of extortion, burglary, gambling, and loansharking, and this put them in direct competition with the Lotus and the Red Eagles.

Gang problems had been growing in Vancouver for years. Two years before the Ming kidnapping, Chinese engineer Johnson Ting was abducted by gang members and held captive for six days while his wife tried to raise $300,000. Ting was freed after police raided a Kingsway motel room and rescued him. In October 1984 Daniel Da Long Chen, identified as a member of the Red Eagles, pleaded guilty to a charge of extorting money from an employee of a Chinese restaurant at Main Street and Twenty-seventh Avenue.

In *Iced: The Story of Organized Crime in Canada*, author Stephen Schneider notes that the Vancouver Police Department saw an escalation in Asian gang violence around 1984, the year before the Mings were murdered. "At first the weapons of choice were lead pipes and baseball bats. This was followed by an increase in the use of knives and even meat cleavers and machetes," he writes. "Gang members then began using guns."

Smith Reveals Orders to Police: Solve Abduction, Quash Gangs

In March 1985 BC's Attorney General Brian Smith held a press conference to say that solving the kidnapping and murder of Jimmy and Lily Ming and breaking up Asian youth gangs were the top law-enforcement priorities. "For a number of months, there has been a very concerted police task force in Vancouver working on nothing but this problem," said Smith. The task force was concentrating on the activities of the Red Eagles, Lotus, and Viet Ching gangs.

Mayor Mike Harcourt branded Vietnamese gangs as "public enemy number one" and urged gang members to get out of Vancouver before the authorities chased them out. "They think we're weak-kneed and they laugh at us. Well, they're not going to laugh for long," said Harcourt. The mayor's tough-talking rhetoric did little to appease the citizens of Vancouver, and the Vietnamese community objected to being targeted this way. Some of them took great offence and held a demonstration the next day.

Gang members don't usually enjoy long lives. They often take care of any grievances themselves, rather than go to police, using what SFU's Robert Gordon calls "extrajudicial resolution methods."

In January 1987 a rash of armed robberies ended with the shooting of a fourteen-year-old member of the Lotus gang in the Golden Princess Theatre (now the Rio), on East Broadway. Tony Hong was watching *All the Wrong Clues* with friends when he was shot in the head by William Yeung, a sixteen-year-old member of the Viet Ching gang, who was carrying a .38-calibre gun. Hong survived but lost his eye.

Yeung, who had moved to Canada with his family in 1976, said in court that he was working his way into the gang through shoplifting, vandalism, and swinging a baseball bat in fights with rival gangs. The full price of admission was to shoot a rival gang member. He was told that the gang members would intimidate any witnesses from the theatre into not testifying, he would get three years at most, and he would be able to learn English while in the penitentiary. Unfortunately for Yeung, his case was moved up to adult court, the gang members reneged on their promises, and he was sentenced to eight years. He was released on day parole to a half-way house and then deported in 1993.

By 1990, when Ngoc Tung Dang, a gunman for the Red Eagles gang, was murdered in his car, police reported that gang violence was ramping up, with driveby shootings becoming almost routine. SFU's Gordon notes that the most popular and effective silencer for this method of murder is a turnip.

The Ming family did all they could to bring Jimmy and Lily back alive. They closed the Yangtse Kitchen and attempted to sell it to raise the ransom. They were unsuccessful, and they reopened the restaurant in July 1985. "We could have sold everything we had and still not raised enough money," Harry Ming, the youngest brother, told a reporter. "I grew up with my father cooking in a restaurant. This is what we do. We are not afraid. We are not going to walk away from all we have put into this business."

Despite rewards totalling more than $22,000 and a special police task force consisting of eight full-time Vancouver Police detectives and another four part-time officers from the RCMP in Squamish to solve the murders, the killers of Jimmy and Lily Ming were never found.

Sources:
Chinatown News: March 18, 1985
Globe and Mail: March 13, 1985
Province: March 12, 1985; April 29, 1990; December 10, 1993
Squamish Times: March 19, 1985
Vancouver Sun: March 12, 13, 14, 19, 20, 28; April 18; May 22; July 11; August 17, 1985; January 26, 1987

"There is no shortage of opportunities for white-collar psychopaths that think big," wrote Dr. Robert Hare in Without Conscience: The Disturbing World of the Psychopaths Among Us. *"If I were unable to study psychopaths in prison, my next choice would very likely be a place like the Vancouver Stock Exchange."*

CHAPTER 17

Missing without a Trace

Lisa Masee worked at the Yokoi Hair Salon on Cambie Street in Vancouver's South Cambie neighbourhood. She'd met her husband Nick there, and she was known as a punctual, hard-working employee. So when she failed to turn up one morning in August 1994, her boss Shige Yokoi called Lisa's sister, Loretta Mo Kuen Leung.

The last time anyone had heard from Lisa was when she'd called the salon to say that something had come up and she wouldn't be coming in the next day. "She was telling me about some kind of court case that suddenly came up, and she couldn't come to work," Yokoi told a reporter. "I understood she would be back to work on Tuesday."

Tuesday arrived, but Lisa didn't. When no one answered the phone at the Masees' North Vancouver house, Loretta went over to check. Nick Masee was security conscious, but Lisa found the door unlocked, the security system off, and the couple's Chrysler LeBaron convertible parked in the carport. Spider, the Masees' seventeen-year-old Persian cat, had been left inside without food. The Masees' passports were in the house. Two plastic ties, similar to the ones that police use for handcuffs, were found just inside the front entrance. Loretta filed a report with the North Vancouver RCMP.

Eve Lazarus photo, 2015

Nick and Lisa Masee's house on Monteray Avenue in North Vancouver.

Ex-banker Had Ties to Shady Characters

Nick Masee had retired from his job as head of private banking with the Bank of Montreal eight months before the couple disappeared. He'd worked with the bank for thirty-five years and was the private banker for some of the Vancouver Stock Exchange's most colourful stock promoters, regularly socializing with high-rollers such as Murray Pezim, Harry Moll, Nelson Skalbania, and Herb Capozzi. Nick dined with them at Hy's, Il Giardino, and Chardonnay's, some of Vancouver's most exclusive restaurants. He went on weekend fishing trips to the luxurious Sonora Lodge. He flew in private jets to boxing matches in Las Vegas and stayed at his friends' Scottsdale, Arizona, mansions, and was a guest at one of Murray Pezim's weddings on a $3-million luxury yacht. And, as a director of Ballet BC, Nick regularly organized fundraising events. At the time of his disappearance, he served as president of the Netherlands Businessmens and Professionals Association. "He enjoyed the Howe Street life," his son told *Vancouver Sun* reporter David Baines. "I don't think there's any secret to that."

Nick knew his way around the Vancouver Stock Exchange, and he was known to invest in his clients' deals. One of the biggest players on the VSE was Harry Moll, who was infamous as the boss of the Pineridge Capital Group. The company ran several sketchy VSE start-ups including Cross Pacific Pearls, which Moll touted would grow the world's biggest pearl in a Honolulu shopping centre. (It didn't.) Pineridge imploded in 1992 and sparked one of many government inquiries into the VSE. Moll was turfed out of the Exchange and took up residence in the Grand Cayman Islands.

Murray Pezim, another of Nick's clients, had lost as many fortunes as he had made. Probably the most colourful promoter to hit the VSE, he was the brains behind the Hemlo property and the Vita Pez Rejuvenation Pills scheme. At one time, Pezim owned the BC Lions football team.

Another of Nick's associates from his banking days and a frequent tennis partner was Nelson Skalbania, a flamboyant promoter who at one point owned a $2.7-million de Havilland jet, a luxury yacht called Chimon, the Montreal Alouettes football club, the Vancouver Canadians baseball club, and the Edmonton Oilers hockey club (though not at the same time).

At the time the Masees went missing, Skalbania was on trial for stealing $100,000 from a former business associate's trust fund. Nick was scheduled to testify as a witness for the prosecution. Police told reporters that he was only a minor witness and did not believe that the court proceedings had anything to do with the disappearance of the Masees.

Vancouver Sun, November 14, 1991 (photo by Malcolm Parry)

Nick and Lisa Masee at a Ballet BC party, November 1991.

Living Beyond Means

Nick certainly looked the part of the successful businessman. At fifty-five, he was a trim five-foot-seven, with a perpetual tan, gold jewellery, greying blond hair, blue eyes, and an attractive second wife sixteen years his junior.

But while the Masees may have associated with the rich and powerful, they were living way beyond their means. As a banker, Nick pulled in around $85,000 a year. Their modest North Vancouver home was heavily mortgaged, and they owed $70,000 on their credit cards. Lisa had a full-time job as a hairdresser, and unlike their jet-setting contemporaries, Nick and Lisa's getaway was a time-share in Maui.

Nick was born in the Netherlands, where he'd been a top ranking junior tennis player. He had two children from his first marriage—Nick Jr, who at the time of his father and stepmother's disappearance was an executive with a moving company in Singapore, and Tanya, who lived in Holland.

Nick was banking that his new venture as a director of a VSE start-up called Turbodyne Technologies would propel him into the big leagues. Turbodyne was developing a device to cut emissions from diesel engines, and it was Nick's job to look after the corporate budget and set up evaluations for the company's anti-pollution device.

VSE Promoters a Dying Breed

Before disappearing in 1999, the Vancouver Stock Exchange boasted that it was the third major stock exchange in Canada, raising a billion dollars in venture capital. In fact, it was little more than a legalized gambling joint in which, according to a 1979 study commissioned for the BC Government, investors in the exchange lost eighty-four percent of their money some of the time and all of their money forty percent of the time. Scams were numerous and usually involved shell companies that ranged from a mining company that became an official bat sanctuary before going into real estate to a video vending machine company that transformed into a bio-medical outfit, to various fictitious gold mines. The brokers and the promoters raked in huge amounts of money, and the exchange attracted capital from all sorts of sources, including arms dealers, drug lords, biker gangs, and organized crime. Connections to the exchange were often lethal. In the 1980s and '90s, a lot of people involved with Vancouver's Howe Street stock scene went missing or showed up dead:

- In March 1987 VSE promoter Guy Lamarche was shot to death in Toronto's Royal York Hotel.

- In May 1990 John Ramon (Ray) Ginnetti, a forty-eight-year-old Howe Street broker, was shot in the head inside his tony West Vancouver home, his body found stuffed in a closet. Ginnetti was rumoured to be selling stock for a mineral exploration company that had gang connections, and his funeral was attended by a mixture of business people and bikers.

- In April 1991 Fred Hofman, church treasurer and former VSE player, disappeared after bilking his victims out of $10 million in a Ponzi scheme.

- In August 1996 Terrance Watts, a forty-one-year-old former broker with a history of shady stock deals, was found dead in Chinatown. He had been shot and his body stuffed into the trunk of his car.

• In January 1997 David Ward was found dead in his Nissan Pathfinder. Like Watts and Ginnetti, Ward was shot in the head, gangland-style. His vehicle was double parked on East Pender Street, near Playland, the engine was still running, his money and jewellery untouched. Ward had been convicted of stock manipulation and making secret commission payments totalling more than $15 million. He served eight months of a three-year sentence. Rumours circulated that he was involved with drugs and that he had managed to hide millions in secret offshore accounts before forensic accountants recovered about $5 million.

Leon Nowek, Masee's partner in Turbodyne Technologies, was the last person to hear from the Masees on the day that they went missing. Strangely, it was Lisa who called him at 10:00 a.m. to say they were going away for a few days and that Nick would phone him later. Shortly before calling Nowek, Lisa had phoned the hair salon where she worked to tell them she wouldn't be in the next day, but would see them the following Tuesday. Lisa used Nick's cell phone to make the calls.

On the day before their disappearance, Lisa had told a friend whom she worked with that a man from California had contacted Nick about a possible business deal. He had told Nick that they'd met when he worked at the Bank of Montreal and that he had $10 million that he wanted to invest. The man said he was interested in Turbodyne Technologies. He apparently told Nick that he'd send a limo to his house, and they would have dinner at Trader Vic's, a well-known haunt for Howe Street denizens and a favourite restaurant of the Masees. No record was ever found of a limo rental sent to the Masee address.

Lisa was skeptical, her friend Teresa Pham later told *Vancouver Sun* reporter David Baines. A businessman with $10 million that he didn't know what to do with? That struck Lisa as "pretty weird." But Nick phoned Trader Vic's and booked a table for four for dinner at 8:30 p.m. Tommy Chang supervised the dining room and knew the Masees well. He reserved a window seat that looked over Coal Harbour and the North Shore mountains. Nick called to say they would be delayed. But when the Masees and their guests hadn't arrived by 9:30 p.m., Chang gave away their table. "I was surprised," Chang told reporter Baines. "He's always punctual when he had a reservation."

Next to the immediate family, only Nick's friend Walter Davidson, a former Social Credit MLA and speaker of the legislature, seemed concerned that the Masees were missing. Davidson told reporters he wouldn't answer their questions because he was scared for his life.

There was some evidence that Nick and Lisa were on the lam. The Masees had taken a mysterious trip to the Cayman Islands the April before their disappearance, uncharacteristically not telling anyone where they were going. According to a private detective hired by Nick Masee Jr, the Masees had set up a bank account in the Caymans with $50,000 worth of stock. The CBC reported that they had wills drawn up while they were there.

Parallels were drawn with Fred Hofman, another missing Dutchman who belonged to the same association as Nick, and whom Nick had inadvertently introduced to other members of Metro Vancouver's Dutch Community. Hofman returned the favour by stealing and then running off with their money.

On the other hand, there was also plenty of evidence that the Masees did not leave voluntarily. Lisa was about to celebrate her fortieth birthday in just a few weeks, and her colleagues at the hair salon had planned a weekend away in Whistler. She was also to be a bridesmaid at her cousin's wedding. Nick Jr passed a lie detector test in which he denied having any contact with his father.

"No Street Smarts," Says Pezim

"[Nick] knew everything about the street, but he had no street smarts," Murray Pezim told the *Vancouver Sun*'s Baines. "He might have got himself into the wrong place at the wrong time." Pezim said that while he didn't know if Nick's disappearance was connected to the VSE, "I'll tell you one thing: number one, it's money."

Herb Capozzi, another of the former banker's clients, said: "He's straight as an arrow. He's the kind of guy that if he won money in a poker game, he would claim it on his income tax."

Unsubstantiated rumours began circulating that Nick had guaranteed Harry Moll's gambling debts, and those debts were sold to a local biker gang. A variation on that theme went that Nick might have either deliberately or accidently become involved with laundering a motorcycle gang's drug money. Masee's children believe he's dead. Nick Jr told the *Globe and Mail* that his father lacked the bravado and ruthlessness needed to stage a phony death. He was strait-laced and conservative and took few risks, he said. In 2001 he and his sister Tanya petitioned the BC Supreme Court to have their father declared dead. "My father was always a very open man who enjoyed sharing details of what was happening in his life and work," Tanya said in a court statement. "However, in the six months before his disappearance, he became very guarded about his life and, in particular, the details of his work. Furthermore, he seemed concerned for his safety."

If they did a runner, or as another rumour suggested, entered a witness protection program, they left without a trace. Their passports were left in the house, and their bank accounts and credit cards remained unused. Leaving the family cat behind would have been a cruel but convincing touch.

North Vancouver RCMP Corporal Gord Reid is keeping an open mind. "It's a head-scratcher. I've got missing people that I assume are murdered because they are not the kind of people who would be able to disappear. But the Masees could. He was a sophisticated guy. They both had passports from other countries, they had lived around the world. He understood international banking, and they had some money stashed aside. If [they] wanted to disappear, they would be much better equipped to do it than most people," he says. "Generally speaking, if organized criminals want to gun you down, they don't do it so cleanly, and it's not two people who disappear at once, so that [suggests that] they made themselves go missing. But there are other things that [imply that] maybe somebody had a problem. I just don't know, I really don't."

One of the first things investigators looked at after the Masees went missing was Nick's company, Turbodyne Technologies, a controversial company on the stock market. "Turbodyne Technologies had purported to develop some new engine technology that was going to cut in half the world's requirement for fossil fuel, and they were going to make bazillions of dollars. It didn't work out, people lost money—and Nick Masee was representing them."

After 2003 all North Vancouver homicides went to IHIT, the Integrated Homicide Investigation Team based in Surrey. At that time, the North Vancouver RCMP detachment had around fifty cold case missing person investigations and seventeen unsolved homicides dating back to 1964.

The Masees remain one of North Vancouver RCMP's biggest missing person cases. It sits inside four cardboard banker boxes that contain details of the twenty-year-old mystery, including interviews with associates, banking records, travel records, photos of their house, documents found inside the house, and photographs of the couple.

Sources:
Equity Magazine: October 1995
Financial Post: February 1, 1997
Forbes Magazine: May 29, 1989
Globe and Mail: July 25, October 4, 1995; February 20, 1997; October 15, 2001
News 1130: August 2014
Northern Miner: May 4–10, 1998
North Shore News: August 15, 2014
North Shore Outlook: August 9, 2012
Province: August 13, 2014
Report on Business: August 25, 2014
Silicon Investor: February 3, April 29, 1997
Vancouver Sun: August 27, 30; September 3, 1994; December 16, 1995; January 17, 1997; June 7, 2002; August 13, 2014

"It drives me mad when I see on the news that somebody was murdered thirty-six years ago and they've got the guy through DNA," says Carol Rogier. *"Here I'm thinking, well, what about Muriel? She was not a throw-away person. She was not."*

CHAPTER 18

Murder in Mole Hill

Muriel Lindsay was feeling good about her life. She had a well-paid job at the post office where she'd made a number of friends, and a little over a year earlier, she had fought a battle against non-Hodgkin's lymphoma and survived. But she found it strange to look in the mirror. Her big blue eyes were still the most prominent feature of her face, but her long blonde hair had grown back dark and curly after the chemo, and she wore it short for the first time.

Muriel spent Valentine's Day in 1996 with her mother Marjorie and cousin Carol Rogier. They had lunch on Granville Island, and she told them how excited she was about moving out of the Comox Street boarding house where she'd lived for thirteen years. She'd signed the lease on a one-bedroom apartment on Beach Avenue with a view of English Bay, where she was moving at the end of the month. Most of her things were already packed. Over lunch, she planned to choose a colour for the new carpet that her cousin Carol and her husband were installing as a home-warming present for her.

She never made it to her new apartment. Two days after she was supposed to move, Muriel Lindsay was found beaten to death in her room, just a block from St. Paul's Hospital where she had been born in 1956.

Courtesy Kent Lindsay

Muriel Lindsay at St Paul's Hospital while waiting for cancer treatment, ca. 1990s.

Courtesy Kent Lindsay

Kent, Marjorie, Muriel, and Eric Lindsay at their West Vancouver home, late 1950s.

Muriel grew up in the exclusive British Properties area of West Vancouver. Her father Eric Lindsay was a celebrity photographer and reporter for the *Vancouver Sun*, and her mother Marjorie stayed home to look after Muriel and her older brother Kent. Muriel's biggest influence growing up was her grandmother Muriel May, a successful realtor who had the exclusive rights to sell property for the British Pacific Properties in the 1950s and was a shareholder of West Vancouver's Panorama Film Studios. (The studio produced movies such as *Carnal Knowledge*, *McCabe and Mrs. Miller,* and the television series, *The Littlest Hobo*.) Kent and Muriel were raised with a lot of love and care. The kids learned to swim and to sail, took art classes, and spent plenty of time outdoors.

"She was a happy kid," says Kent. "She really looked up to me, and she liked to follow me around. She would fall on her bottom and then bounce a couple of times when she was learning to walk, so we called her Sissy Boom Boom."

Muriel and Kent went to Westcott Elementary and later to Pauline Johnson. Marjorie talked Eric into selling their rancher and moving to a two-bedroom apartment in a new luxury building by the ocean, dubbed "the pink palace."

Move to Toronto
Shortly after the move, Eric was offered a job writing television news for CBC's *The National*, and after a year of separation, Marjorie reluctantly joined him in Toronto and enrolled the kids at Jessie Ketchum high school.

Two years later, things started to unravel quickly. Eric and Marjorie split up for the second and last time. Kent and then Marjorie moved back to West Vancouver to live with Marjorie's mother, while Eric and Muriel stayed in Toronto. Muriel, now fourteen, was taken out of Jessie Ketchum, a public school in the Yorkville area of Toronto, and put into Branksome Hall, a swanky private school for girls in Toronto's upmarket Rosedale.

Being separated from her mother, grandmother, and brother was particularly hard for Muriel. She was close in age to her Oshawa cousin Barb (Lindsay) Kneteman, and Barb remembers her when she first moved to Toronto as a bright and happy twelve-year-old.

"She was about five-foot-seven, and she had really pretty blonde hair that she always wore straight in the middle. The first thing you noticed about her was her eyes because they were so big," says Barb. "She liked to be active and she liked music and dancing and she loved to sing. We went to day-camp, and she was very talkative and friendly. But coming from Vancouver, Oshawa must have been a big let-down for her."

Muriel bounced back and forth between her parents, finished school in Toronto, and lived there for the next six years. Her parents' split had hit her hard, though, and by the time she was eighteen her friends and family were noticing that the once happy, extroverted girl was undergoing a personality change. Muriel broke up with her boyfriend and had a nervous breakdown. She was diagnosed as a borderline psychotic, and her mother stepped in and brought her back to Vancouver.

"She was a gentle, kind soul. We always thought of her as a kid because she was very young and very immature for her age," says her cousin Carol. "She was quite close to Kent, relatively on and off with her mother, and very close to her grandmother, who basically raised Kent and Muriel once their parents split."

Muriel's mental health stabilized once she was back with her mother and grandmother. "I know that she really missed Vancouver when she was in Toronto, so I wasn't surprised when she went back there," says Barb. She remembers visiting Muriel in a boarding house on Davie Street in the mid-1970s. "She knew Vancouver, and she loved it.

Courtesy Kent Lindsay

A young Muriel Lindsay.

She loved hanging out at the beach, and she knew lots of people. She was a real Vancouver kid, that's for sure; that was her comfort zone. She knew how to get around in a city. She was not afraid, she was not a timid girl at all."

Vancouver's West End

In 1983 Muriel moved into a room in a heritage house in Mole Hill, part of Vancouver's West End. It was run by an elderly lady known to everyone as "Mrs Henry." Like many of the single-family homes built in the early years of the twentieth century, the house had been modified into a boarding house in the 1940s. Muriel had a room on the second floor above the entry, and it suited her well. The rent was inexpensive, she loved the West End, and she was allowed to keep her two cats there.

When Muriel was hired by Canada Post as a letter sorter, she could walk to work. For the first time, Muriel had a job that paid decently and came with benefits. She could think of saving for the future and moving to a place of her own. "It was a dream job for her. She really liked it, and she met some good people there," says Kent.

But while things were finally picking up for Muriel, there were some disturbing events in the months leading up to her death. She'd complained to her family that two men who lived in the boarding house had bothered her on different occasions.

In a letter to her father written shortly before her murder, Muriel wrote: "My crazy neighbour is back and now another nightmare. I can't find another pair of jeans. I think I'll get a new lock on my door and won't give Mrs Henry a key. She has those two guys for dinner on Sundays. I think they might have stolen my key and got a duplicate. One night my door opened. I looked out and Juan was

walking down the stairs. I am not just paranoid am I? I shall do that with a new lock. This is not good, 3.00 a.m. or so. What a creep!"

Carol said that Muriel had complained to her too about Juan. She said that he often harassed her verbally and that she was afraid of him. She told her brother Kent that one of her beloved cats had gone missing and she thought that someone had kidnapped it.

Eve Lazarus photo, 2015

The Comox Street house where Muriel was murdered in 1996.

My crazy neighbour is back and now another nightmare. I can't find another pair of jeans. I think I'll get a new lock on my door and won't give Mrs. Henry a key. She has those 2 guys for dinner on Sundays. I think they might have stolen my key and got a duplicate. One night my door opened. I looked out and Juan was walking down the stairs. I am not just paranoid am I? I shall do that with a new lock. This is not good, 3 AM or so. What a creep! I better go get lunch now. Then I'm off to do the stores.

Hope all is well with you.

Love Muriel.

PS.

Marg is going on a new coding machine on Monday. VES. "Vision Encoding System." They're training her for 4 hours a night, Computer keys etc, sitting down. Neat aye?

The province and the Sun were on strike all week. They're back today

Courtesy Kent Lindsay

Part of a chilling letter Muriel sent to her father shortly before her murder in February 1996.

Bizarre Poison Pen Letters

Muriel was also receiving strange letters and was disturbed enough by them to have all her mail forwarded to her mother's apartment in West Vancouver. A bizarre handwritten letter sent to Muriel just three weeks before her death started with the words "Hi Scum. You are now 40. We hope and pray that you start acting like an adult and not like a teenager. We also hope you stop smoking. You stink." Marjorie Lindsay was upset when she opened and read the letter, but after discussing it with Eric, she decided not to show it to Muriel. It was a decision she regretted.

On the day after Valentine's Day, Muriel worked the afternoon shift at the main post office on West Georgia Street, finishing at 11:00 p.m. As they did most nights, Muriel and a co-worker walked through downtown Vancouver to their homes in the West End. The two parted company when they reached Muriel's house.

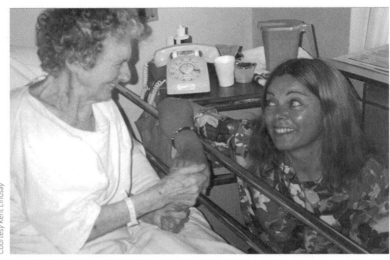
Muriel visiting her grandmother in Oshawa in 1992.

Muriel and Marjorie spoke on the phone every day, so when Marjorie repeatedly failed to reach her daughter, she started to worry. Marjorie and a friend drove to Muriel's place on the Saturday afternoon. They got a key to her apartment from the landlady.

"They went right up into her room and found her lying there dead," says Kent.

Police believe the time of death was around 12:15 a.m. on Friday, February 16. She died from blows to her head and larynx.

Did Muriel Have a Stalker?

Kent believes that his sister had a stalker and says it's possible that he let himself in through the back fire-escape door, which was often left ajar by tenants. "People would go out that way instead of out the front door. They all knew they were supposed to leave it locked, but I guess that night it was open, and he waited for her," says Kent. "The police figure he snuck in behind the door that was ajar and killed her."

A few days after her death, police were in the apartment searching for evidence and pulled out the fridge. They found Muriel's little orange and white cat, Morris, hiding there. Marjorie took him home.

"It just makes me crazy to think that this guy got away with murder," says her friend Carol Rogier. "Has he done it again?"

Says Kent: "I'd never felt such pain in all my life. When somebody is yanked away from your life suddenly, it's really, really hard."

Muriel Lindsay wasn't the only member of her family to suffer a violent death. When her great-grandfather Detective Richard Levis was shot to death in August 1914, he became the fourth Vancouver police officer killed in the line of duty. Levis was investigating a stabbing. The suspect, known to police as "Mickey the Dago," had stabbed another man in a fight at a café. When Levis and his partner searched Mickey's shack on Alexander Street, Levis found him hiding in the bedroom, armed with a sawed off shotgun. Levis died from gunshot wounds to his chest two days later.

Detective Richard Levis, killed in the line of duty, 1914.

Courtesy Vancouver Police Museum

Levis, only twenty-eight at the time of his death, left his wife Estelle with three children—Cyril, Muriel (May), and Carroll—all under the age of five. Shortly after her husband's death, Estelle was hired as a matron in the women's division of the Vancouver Police Department and worked there until 1919 when she married fellow officer John McLellan.

Carol Rogier has fond memories of her grandmother. "She was a five-foot-tall Irish whippersnapper. She worked 6:00 p.m. to 6:00 a.m., six days a week with three little kids at home," she says. "She was an absolutely amazing woman, and she wasn't afraid of anything."

Carol's father, Cyril Levis, was an actor, and with his brother, Carroll Richard Levis, moved the family to England. Carroll had a long career in radio and television at the BBC and became quite famous in the 1940s and '50s, at one point hosting his own television program called *The Carroll Levis Discovery Show*, a talent show for young people.

There were several possible suspects, and police looked carefully at the other residents of the Comox Street house. Juan, the man who caused Muriel such concern, returned to Mexico shortly after her murder, and as far as the family is aware, remains a suspect.

Muriel's funeral was held at the Hollyburn Funeral Home in West Vancouver. Carol says that many of her co-workers from the post office attended the funeral and raised $12,000 to donate to cancer research in her name. Some of her co-workers told Carol that they had no idea that she had gone through cancer. "They said she would wear a baseball hat backwards, and they just thought that was her style. Nobody ever knew; she kept everything very close to her heart," says Carol. "The saddest thing of all is that [in unsolved murder cases], families don't have any closure. What we really want is some sort of restitution for what happened."

Source:
Vancouver Sun: February 20, 1996; February 8, 1997; February 3, 2006

"Six years has gone by, and he thinks he's got away with murder," says former Provincial Unsolved Homicide Unit detective Steve McCartney. "That's the part I loved about my job. I loved the fact that these individuals thought they got away with it, and they were living their lives having forgotten about the victims. And what I really liked was showing up one day with an arrest warrant or just to jerk their chains a bit, knowing that one day I was coming back."

CHAPTER 19

To Catch a Killer: Anatomy of a Cold Case

Vancouver 2005

Brian Townsend was in need of a fix and some easy money, and Vancouver's Davie Street seemed as good a place as any to find it. When he saw a woman walking down the street, distracted by the shop windows, he swooped in, grabbed her purse, and took off up Davie, trying to lose himself in the crowd. Unfortunately for Townsend, a police officer on patrol in the West End saw the robbery, gave chase, and arrested him.

Townsend was taken to the station, fingerprinted, and placed in a cell. The next morning, the fifty-one-year-old appeared before a judge, received a future court date, and was released. As a matter of course, his prints were sent off to the Canadian Criminal Real Time Identification Services in Ottawa for processing. Townsend was a small-time criminal and crack addict who lived in Vancouver's Downtown Eastside and survived on a disability pension and what he could steal. He'd been picked up by police for small offences but had managed to get away with an appearance notice and a couple of arrest warrants. His fingerprints had never entered the system.

Now, with the theft of a purse, Townsend's prints would help police close a five-year-old murder case.

Courtesy Bruyère Morzuch

Vivien Morzuch, age twelve.

Kamloops 2000

Fifteen-year-old Vivien Morzuch was a slim, blond, blue-eyed boy who played bass guitar. He was born in France but raised in Montreal by his mother after his parents separated when he was five. Vivien grew into a troubled teen who started to act out. When he ran away to Toronto in April 2000, his mother filed a missing person's report.

Not long after he arrived in Toronto, he was arrested for marijuana possession. Although it was a minor drug arrest, he was already on the police database as a runaway with an outstanding arrest warrant. His parents, who were both in France at the time of his arrest, were told that Vivien would be kept in custody at a youth detention centre in Ontario until they arrived to pick him up. But instead of holding the teen, police dropped the charges and released him. The Salvation Army paid for a bus ticket to take him back to Montreal

As his father Frank Morzuch, a visual artist, later told a reporter: "He was put on the street without a penny. If parents had done that, they would have been put in jail."

Once out on the street in Toronto, Vivien decided not to use the ticket to Montreal. He called his mother from a payphone and told her he was heading to BC to find work as a fruit picker and to practice his English.

"He was not bad. He was a dreamer, and he was not conscious of danger," Vivien's mother Françoise Langlade told a reporter a few months later. "Everybody loved him. I loved him."

She said that Vivien was impatient to grow up. He was interested in spirituality and had told her that he wanted to go to Asia and live in a Buddhist monastery. "He wanted everything too soon," she said. Vivien travelled with some French Canadians that he met along the way. He and Lucien Leblanc, nineteen, met in Banff, Alberta and hitchhiked together to Kelowna, BC. Once in Kelowna, they pooled their money—probably whatever Vivien had left from selling the bus ticket—and bought about twenty-five dollars each of marijuana and magic mushrooms. The boys camped one night in an orchard near Westbank, just outside of Kelowna. The last time Vivien was seen alive, he was panhandling on Victoria Street, the main street in downtown Kamloops, BC.

Two days later, his body was discovered by a couple driving past the Steelhead campground, about twenty-five (forty km) west of Kamloops. He was covered in blood and had been dumped in a ditch near the entrance of the provincial park. Vivien had been beaten to death, his skull fractured by five blows to the top of his head. His body had been in the ditch for at least twenty-four hours. Vivien's body was lying face up, dressed only in plaid boxer shorts and a T-shirt.

Courtesy Bruyère Morzuch

Campsite where Vivien Morzuch was dumped in 2000 just outside Kamloops.

This became part of the hold-back evidence that would eventually help catch his killer.

Because there was no identification on his body, police identified him through his fingerprints. His parents learned of his death through the media.

The murder sparked a massive investigation. Kamloops RCMP conducted more than 500 interviews and generated 250 tips. The only evidence they had to go on was a piece of bloody silver duct tape found near his body with a partial thumbprint and some DNA.

The partial print was sent to the Canadian Criminal Real Time Identification Services in Ottawa, where an analyst categorized it along with the thousands of other prints from around the country she had to process. She entered it into the crime scene database, but it failed to generate a match.

Vivien's murder baffled investigators for five years. Then they got a break, with Brian Townsend's failed snatch-and-grab in Vancouver.

Fingerprint Match

By sheer chance, the same analyst in Ottawa who had received the partial print of Vivien Morzuch's killer in 2000 also processed Townsend's prints. And even though she dealt with hundreds of prints every week, the unsolved murder of a fifteen-year-old boy had stayed with her. She noticed enough of a similarity to compare Townsend's prints with the partial thumbprint that she'd processed five years before. While it wasn't close enough for a positive identification, the analyst felt that it was still worth sending her findings back to the investigator in Kamloops. Her decision set off a chain of events that would help solve Vivien's murder.

The investigator in Kamloops agreed that the prints were close enough to warrant reinvestigating the case. He contacted Steve McCartney, a detective with the Provincial Unsolved Homicide Unit, based in Surrey. McCartney was keen to take on the case. He felt it was solvable, and police were always particularly motivated when it came to catching child killers. "We do consider the victimology. If you have a young child, officers are very interested in the case," he says. McCartney says that, in deciding whether to reinvestigate a cold case, police officers look at the potential for new evidence and if there is forensic evidence that can be tested for DNA. "For instance," he says, "We might have a fingerprint ... but now we know that we can take that fingerprint in certain circumstances, swab it, and get a DNA imprint." Police had a partial fingerprint and DNA from an unknown person on the duct tape found near Vivien's body, which also had Vivien's DNA on it.

McCartney said police believed that the unknown partial print and the unknown DNA belonged to the same person. When they matched Townsend's prints to the partial print on the duct tape, police were able to establish a linkage. But because it was still not enough evidence to legally compel Townsend to give up his DNA, McCartney launched an undercover investigation to covertly follow Townsend and attempt to recover something he discarded to get a sample of his DNA.

Getting DNA

The plan, explained McCartney, was to get his DNA from a cigarette butt, saliva on a coffee cup, or skin cells left behind on a piece of paper or item of clothing that they could compare to the DNA found at the murder scene.

The problem was that Townsend would go from his lodgings at the Union Gospel on East Hastings in Vancouver's Downtown Eastside and smoke crack in a back alley with other junkies. The police couldn't get close enough to get any kind of sample without being noticed.

McCartney says detectives spent two weeks following Townsend, watched him steal bikes, break into cars, and sell stolen property—all offences too small to get a warrant that would force him to provide DNA. At one point, a frustrated undercover detective on the detail got in front of Townsend and dropped some cigarettes on the ground behind him. Townsend, who doesn't smoke cigarettes, didn't even look down.

Then one day, detectives caught an unlikely break. They watched as Townsend went into the old Main Street police station. He was applying for a volunteer job to work with the elderly, and he needed a criminal record check. The line-up was long, the service slow, and detectives watched as Townsend became increasingly frustrated. After a time, he filled out the form, handed it to the clerk, and left. While the form had been handled by people other than Townsend and was useless as a DNA repository, it did give McCartney an idea, one that he had seen used in his days as a detective in sex crimes a few years before. McCartney drew up a mock customer service survey, put an official crest on top, printed it, and had it signed by the chief of police. The accompanying letter told Townsend that if he filled out the survey within two weeks, he would get a free dinner at a local restaurant. McCartney placed the survey inside an envelope with a stamped self-addressed envelope for its return and waited.

Asked about the legality of the survey and the ethics involved, McCartney says: "That's not a dirty trick, that's a trick," he says. "There's a distinction. Dirty tricks are something that would shock the community—something like posing as a priest. But posing as a person taking a survey, I don't think that would shock the community."

Adds Stu Wyatt, a forensic identification expert: "The reason is that [the suspect] gets the survey, and it's totally up to him whether he sends it back or not. The law of entrapment in Canada says police can provide the opportunity, but they can't go beyond that."

Townsend sent back the survey, complaining of slow service. Police continued to tail Townsend and followed him to an alley where they found him selling video cassettes that they had seen him steal from a car. A scruffy-looking undercover detective offered to buy the baseball cap he was wearing, and after some haggling, Townsend sold it to him. Carefully, the officer took the cap out to the street, where another detective waited with a plastic evidence bag.

The survey and the cap were sent to the lab for DNA testing. It was determined that they matched the DNA left on the duct tape at the crime scene five years before. "The estimated probability was that it was a one in forty-eight billion chance that the DNA did not belong to him," said Wyatt. Adds McCartney: "We were ecstatic. This said that the DNA on that duct tape is the same guy who licked the envelope and whose DNA was on the hat. We can say that the DNA belongs to him."

Now that they had a fingerprint and a DNA match, they could request a warrant to compel him to provide a DNA sample. But, says McCartney, it was still not enough to convict Townsend for murder. "He could go to court and say, 'Your Honour, I have a friend, and he's from Kamloops and I got that hat off him, and while he was visiting he filled out that form and licked it,'" says McCartney. "That's reasonable doubt. We have all this information, but we know he could come up with a story."

Building the Case

Police conducted a background check on Townsend. They discovered that he had served in the navy, but was discharged because of a drinking problem. He managed to clean himself up, get married, and become a devout Christian and a Baptist lay minister. He worked at a food bank in Mission, BC. Later, though, he began to derail again, and this time he got into drugs. He and his wife split up, and Townsend spiralled downward, ending up in Vancouver's Downtown Eastside.

The next step in the investigation was to place Townsend in Kamloops around the time of Vivien's murder. Police sifted back through the initial investigation. Townsend's name didn't come up in the list of tips, he had not committed a crime in Kamloops, and he had not used a credit card there. His address at the time of Vivien's murder was in Mission.

Police found that he had a cell phone with a Rogers account in 2000, and they were able to pull his phone records. While he hadn't made a call from Kamloops, he had made one from Red Deer, Alberta, the day before Vivien's body was found. Kamloops was on the most likely route between Red Deer and Mission. Police had placed Townsend in the vicinity of the murder, but McCartney wanted a confession, and he knew that if he could get Townsend to voluntarily give police the "hold-back" evidence, then along with the fingerprint and DNA evidence, getting a conviction would be a virtual slam-dunk. In this case, the hold-back evidence was the boy's clothing, the positioning of his body, and the nature of his injuries. It had not been released to the media, and aside from a handful of officers working the case, it was information only the killer would know.

Mr Big

McCartney felt that his best chance of getting a full confession from Townsend was to launch a Mr Big operation. This is a controversial procedure that the RCMP have used since the early 1990s to either charge or clear suspects in major cold cases. An undercover police officer acting as a crime boss has the suspect perform what he believes to be a series of illegal activities designed to make the suspect think he is an increasingly important part of the organization. Costs can range anywhere from about $2,000 to $200,000. McCartney, who is now an instructor at the Justice Institute of BC, says that before going forward with a Mr Big operation, investigators consider whether the case might be solved and the potential for the subject to reoffend. And, while the workings of Mr Big cases are now common knowledge, fortunately for the police, the bad guys don't seem to notice. "When the media was talking a lot about our undercover operations, we had a general panic in law enforcement, but I don't think the criminals are getting smarter," he says. "I don't think they are watching *The Fifth Estate* on Friday nights, and I don't think they're reading books like yours."

In the case of Brian Townsend, officers determined that there was potential to reoffend, but most importantly, the case was imminently solveable, and it involved a fifteen-year-old victim. An undercover police officer was tasked with making "a cold approach"—the initial contact with Townsend. The operator waited for Townend to come out of a Vancouver hospital and asked him to help him look for "his boss's friend." He gave Townsend twenty dollars.

After three hours of looking for this fictitious individual, Townsend and the operator went to dinner. The operator asked for Townsend's help the next day. The operator told Townsend that "trust is very important, but it has to be earned," and ripped a fifty-dollar bill in half and told him that he'd get the rest after the work was done. The next day, they resumed the search, and Townsend was introduced to a second police operative whose job it was to develop a friendship with Townsend.

The fake gangsters put Townsend to work, first having him move packages around the Lower Mainland and then involving him in more important "jobs" as he gained their trust. Once, Townsend was taken along on what he thought was a robbery where he watched the undercover police officer jam his gun into the mouth of another officer playing the role of the victim and demand a bag of cash. Townsend was paid varying amounts of money for each "job" and told the operator that he liked the rush of a professional job better than drugs. He attended a high-stakes poker game involving ten officers from the Provincial Unsolved Homicide Unit all posing as members of the criminal organization he thought employed him. The game was staged in a high-end hotel room that required a key card to access. Each of the players came with $11,000 cash, money Townsend was given to count.

Townsend was taken to Montreal and placed into a series of staged scenarios— everything from passing an envelope of cash to a supposedly corrupt customs agent to "breaking into" a police compound to steal a bag from an impounded car. Police set up a break-and-enter at a warehouse that they'd rented for that purpose. Townsend stole a safe that police had purchased at Canadian Tire, broke into it and "stole" a collection of stamps worth thousands of dollars that was owned by an RCMP officer. All were acts designed to emphasize the "gang's" motto of "honesty, loyalty, trust."

The Confession

While Townsend thought he was moving up the ranks of the criminal organization, McCartney's role was to step up the murder investigation. He went to where Townsend was staying and identified himself as a detective with Vancouver homicide. He told Townsend that his name had been identified as a person of interest in the death of Vivien Morzuch at the Steelhead Provincial Park near Kamloops.

"I had thought of a bunch of questions for Brian to give him a chance to tell the truth and his side of the story. I told him what date we were looking at and asked him if he could account for his whereabouts. I told him where we were looking, and he said that he was involved in the church at Maple Ridge and that he ran a soup kitchen."

McCartney made a point of not telling Townsend that Vivien was male, and he purposely didn't give the name the proper French pronunciation, yet Townsend knew McCartney was talking about a boy. When McCartney asked Townsend for his DNA, he refused and said he needed to call his lawyer. Instead he called the police officer he believed was the crime boss.

Townsend was now convinced that he was part of the gang. Members of the "gang" took him to a meeting with the crime boss at the Delta Grand Okanagan Resort and Conference Centre in Kelowna. The meeting was captured on a hidden camera and played back at Townsend's trial. The video shows the undercover mountie telling Townsend that he has contacts in the police force and can help him beat the charge if he tells him everything that happened. "You're the guy who was there. I don't want any bullshit," he tells Townsend.

The video shows Townsend—a grey-haired, heavy-set man lying on a couch in the hotel room—describe how he picked up a hitchhiker at a Husky gas station in Revelstoke when he was travelling to Vancouver from Red Deer in a 1977 motor home. He told the officer that he beat the fifteen-year-old with a baseball bat after the boy tried to rob him and said the boy had "grabbed my package and tried to sexually abuse me.

"I was beating his head with a baseball bat. He was bleeding pretty bad," Townsend said. He drove to a campsite, stripped off most of Vivien's clothes, which he later ditched in Agassiz, and dumped his body in the ditch. Then he gave the officer the rest of the hold-back evidence—what Vivien was wearing and the position of his body.

Townsend was arrested for murder.

The Trial

The trial of Brian Townsend, by then fifty-nine, took place at the Kamloops Law Courts more than seven years after the murder.

Even with Townsend's thumbprint, his DNA on the bloody piece of duct tape found near Vivien's battered body, and the Mr Big confession, it was still a complicated second-degree murder trial. Prosecutor Sarah Firestone called thirty-five witnesses and laid out her case in two parts: the travels of Vivien Morzuch in the weeks leading up to his death, and the elaborate undercover operation by the Provincial Unsolved Homicide Unit years later to get a confession from their chief suspect.

Townsend pleaded not guilty and said that Vivien had tried to rob him after the two had shared a couple of joints and then tried to sexually assault him. "He came up and sat in the passenger seat facing me," Townsend testified. "He was talking about money and he wanted to make some money, and he put his hand on my lap. I know that he was suggesting oral sex for money."

Using the once popular and highly successful "homosexual panic defence," Townsend testified that he had been sexually abused as a child, that he was "scared" and "outraged" at the teen's suggestion, and over-reacted physically. "It was so quick," he said. "I just reacted right there ... I had a small kids' baseball bat under the seat, and I grabbed it and knocked him out. I didn't know what to do." Townsend said the teen eventually came to and tried to attack him again, so he bound him with duct tape. "I didn't want him grabbing me while I was driving," he said.

At the sentencing, Townsend, dressed in a red prison tracksuit, showed no emotion as members of the Morzuch family testified how Vivien's murder had devastated their lives.

"Throughout the trial, the family had to endure all sorts of allegations," Frank Morzuch told a reporter. "The defence did not cease trying to age him; they tried to paint him as a criminal, a thief, a drug addict, and a prostitute."

Fifteen-year-old Vivien Morzuch's murder devastated his parents and siblings, sister Bruyère, who was twenty-four at the time of his death, and brother Colomban, twenty-eight. After learning about her brother's death, Bruyère says her life changed forever. "For seven long years I tried to understand how someone could be so violent and fierce. Now I know Vivien was in the wrong place at the wrong time," she said. "Vivien was always dreaming of travelling, adventure and freedom ... I can still hear his laugh when he was a small child. His laugh brought happiness to the whole family."

Morzuch described how, after he learned of Vivien's murder, he travelled to Kamloops to bring home the body of his dead son. He visited the boy at the funeral home and clipped a lock of hair to take for his mother. "It was difficult to find a sample of hair that was not stained with clotted blood," he said through an interpreter.

Townsend was sentenced to life in prison with no chance of parole for fourteen years.

Sources
Globe and Mail: December 22, 2006
Kamloops This Week: October 7, 11, 22, 2008
Kamloops Daily News: October 8, 16, 17; November 4, 2008
Montreal Gazette: August 3, 2000; October 27, 2008
North Shore Outlook: September 24, 2010
Province: September 29, 2000
Truro Daily News: October 22, 2008

Conclusion

Cold murder cases, or as some police officers like to refer to them, "unresolved" cases, are never closed. The details of the lives and deaths of the people I've written about are active files in Vancouver, North Vancouver, Langley, and Surrey. The names of the police officers on the case files may change, but their desire to solve the murders does not.

My hope is that in writing this book and telling the stories of these individuals, new information may emerge that could help police solve these crimes.

Here's how you can help:

If you know anything about the murders in this book, even the really old ones, you might have a crucial piece of information that could help police solve the case and bring some peace to the victim's families.

As Constable Brian Montague of the Vancouver Police Department notes, sometimes even the smallest things can help.

"There are people out there who, for one reason or another, are holding onto valuable information that would solve these cases. It could be an ex-girlfriend or ex-wife or a friend who holds a valuable piece to the puzzle. Sometimes it's a matter of just reconsidering why they are holding on to that information," he says.

If you have information on these or any other unsolved murder cases, no matter how old, please contact the police. For Vancouver, contact the VPD's non-emergency number 604-717-3321, or in other municipalities contact the RCMP detachment where the murder occurred.

Should you wish to remain anonymous, call BC Crime Stoppers at 1-800-222-8477.

Bibliography

Belshaw, John, ed. *Vancouver Confidential.* Vancouver: Anvil Press, 2014.

Cameron, Stevie. *On the Farm: Robert William Pickton and the Tragic Story of Vancouver's Missing Women.* Toronto: Knopf, 2010.

Clark, Doug. *Dark Paths, Cold Trails: How a Mountie Led the Quest to Link Serial Killers to Their Victims.* Toronto: Harper Collins, 2002.

Gould, Terry. *Paper Fan: The Hunt for Triad Gangster Steven Wong.* Toronto: Random House, 2004.

Lazarus, Eve. *At Home with History: the Untold Secrets of Greater Vancouver's Heritage Homes.* Vancouver: Anvil Press, 2007.

————. *Sensational Vancouver.* Vancouver: Anvil Press, 2014.

Macdonald, Ian, and Betty O'Keefe. *The Mulligan Affair: Top Cop on the Take.* Victoria: Heritage House Publishing, 1997.

McDonald, Glen, and John Kirkwood. *How Come I'm Dead?* Surrey: Hancock House, 1985.

McNicoll, Susan. *British Columbia Murders: Notorious Cases and Unsolved Mysteries.* Calgary: Altitude Publishing, 2003.

Munro, Raymond Z. *The Sky's No Limit.* Toronto: Key Porter Books, 1985.

Schneider, Stephen. *Iced: The Story of Organized Crime in Canada.* Toronto: John Wiley & Sons, 2009.

Swan, Joe. *Police Beat: 24 Vancouver Murders.* Vancouver: Cosmopolitan Publishing, 1991.

Vancouver Police Department Annual Reports: 1947–1958 (Vancouver Police Museum).

Websites:

BC Archives Genealogy: http://search-collections.royalbcmuseum.bc.ca/Genealogy/basicSearch (Death Certificates and vital statistics information)

Statistics Canada, Homicide in Canada, 2013: http://www.statcan.gc.ca/daily-quotidien/141201/dq141201a-eng.htm

The History of Metropolitan Vancouver: http://Vancouverhistory.ca

Vancouver Police Department (annual reports): http://vancouver.ca/police/policeboard/AnnualReport.htm

Vancouver Public Library, city directories: http://vpl.ca/bccd/index.php

Vancouver Sun, obituaries: http://www.legacy.com/obituaries/vancouversun

Index

Eve Lazarus is an award-winning writer with a passion for history. Her previous books include *Sensational Vancouver, Sensational Victoria: Bright Lights, Red Lights, Murders, Ghosts and Gardens,* and *At Home with History: The Untold Secrets of Greater Vancouver's Heritage Homes* (all published by Anvil Press). Eve lives in North Vancouver and blogs obsessively at *evelazarus.com.*